EAST KENT

CANTERBURY AN...

Christine Baldwin

S.B. Publications

First published in 2004 by S. B. Publications
19 Grove Road, Seaford, East Sussex BN25 1TP

Little Hiker Series

Previous Titles
Walks in Ashdown Forest
Walks Around the Coastline of Kent

ISBN 1-85770-288-3

Designed and Typeset by EH Graphics (01273) 515527
Printed by Ethos Productions Ltd.

Front cover photo: *River Stour - by Grove Ferry Pub.*
Back cover photo: *Boardwalk through the reed beds, Stodmarsh Nature Reserve.*
Title page photo: *Canterbury City wall.*

Photographs by Christine Baldwin and Rita Keatley.

CONTENTS

All the walks mentioned have been chosen to represent East Kent's beauty and diversity opening up a tiny corner of England. Please respect the countryside and follow the country code. Carry an OS map for reference, a camera to capture the moment and enjoy your walk in any season.

The Little Hiker series

'The Little Hiker'.
An original woodcarving by Rita Keatley.

ACKNOWLEDGEMENTS

I would like to thank Rita for the use of The Little Hiker and her
contribution to the photographs.

Short History of the Area

The south-east corner of 'The Garden of England' has many surprises and a great deal of historical wealth to show off. Canterbury and Ashford, as well as the surrounding villages, offer both ancient woodlands, nature reserves, historical places of interest along with the hospitality of the people.

The most frequent type of ancient woodland is a dense coppiced area of Hazel, Hornbeam and Sweet Chestnut, along with Oak, as well as the brilliant white flowers of wood anemones and bluebells in spring. In richer soils at the base of valleys Ash and Maple are accompanied by the shiny green leaves of Dog's Mercury covering the woodland floor.

Blean Nature Reserve boasts of its rare species of butterfly like the Heath Fritillary Butterfly and the Duke of Burgundy Butterfly which feed on the common cow wheat and rare heathland areas which support Oval Sedge and Heath Spotted Orchid plants.

Bonsai Bank, part of the Denge Woods walk, is a good site to see the Lady Orchid (each flower looking like a lady dressed in a pink spotted dress and bonnet) and the dwarf or Bonsai Norway Spruce tree after which the area has been named. Stodmarsh Reserve, where the rare Bittern and Bearded Tit birds winter in the scarce areas of reed beds, is where wildlife in all its guises can be seen in varying seasons. Along with the exploration of both the Great Stour river, which was once the 3-mile wide division between Kent and Thanet, is the Little Stour, dug to help drain the area when converting into marshland.

The Crab & Winkle Way takes its name from the first regular passenger steam railway line which ran between Canterbury and Whitstable from May 1830 until it was finally closed in 1953 due to lack of use. The route was opened by the Crab & Winkle Trust in 1999 as a traffic-free path between the two towns using both the old railway line, unspoilt countryside and woodland.

Hothfield Common has the last surviving valley bogs in the county where nature in all its guises is a joy to visit in any season. Ashford has its own oasis of colour and splendour in The Warren. Hamstreet Nature Reserve's woodland has a special significance in that it is the last remnant of an Ice Age forest as well as an area where rare birds and plants are encouraged to flourish. King's Wood is where wooden sculptures and other 'useful' sculptures help create an area of fun, entwined within a natural setting of woodland. Perry Wood allows a small slice of history along with some fantastic views across the Kent Downs to be explored and admired.

And Fordwich, with its historical ties to Canterbury, is a small area of created wilderness which has become a natural habitat for many extraordinary sights.

Map of Complete Walking Area

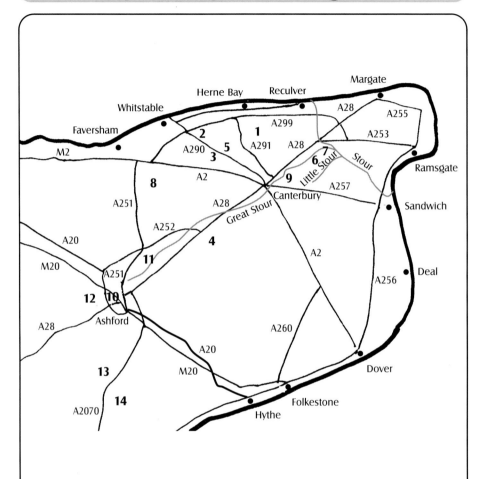

1	East Blean Wood Reserve	8	Perry Wood
2	Clowes Wood	9	Fordwich
3	Blean Wood	10	Ashford Warren
4	Denge/Eggringe Woods	11	King's Wood
5	Crab and Winkle Walk	12	Hothfield Common
6	Stodmarsh Nature Reserve	13	Orlestone Forest
7	The Stours	14	Hamstreet Woods Reserve

Canterbury

From Canterbury's first recorded humble beginnings of 20 B.C., when the area was an Iron Age capital, to the present time, history abounds around every corner. In Roman times Canterbury was a settlement known as Durovernum Cantiacorum. In A.D. 597 St. Augustine and his monks arrived in Thanet and subsequently came to Canterbury chanting 'Let thy anger and wrath be turned away from this city' so allowing the Christian faith to be established here. After Thomas Becket's murder and, later, the Reformation, Canterbury guarded its independence from Kent until the nineteenth century as councillors adopted the motto 'Hail Mother of England'. Canterbury remained England's smallest County Borough until 1974 and still retains its Lord Mayor. All the history in between has moulded this city into the historic wonder seen and admired from every sector. The first city wall was built between A.D. 270-290 made of flint and measuring 10 metres high and 2 metres thick with 6 gateways at Westgate, Northgate, Burgate, Newingate, Worthgate and Ridingate. For years the wall was left to decay, then in the 1370s and 1380s sections of the wall were rebuilt and Westgate, the only surviving tower, was restored. During the 1700s the Pavement Commission began to transform Canterbury by removing the walls and using them to pave the widened streets. Also most of the gates and castle were demolished and used for building new road surfaces and private buildings. What is left is approx an hour and a half walk around the walls of Canterbury, an historic sight not to be missed.

Starting in the Dane John gardens follow the concrete path coming up onto the ramparts passing the Dane John mound (a probable Roman burial mound) and continue along passing four open-backed medieval towers used for defence. Continue along passing over the site of Ridingate, one of seven Roman gates, where Watling Street, the Roman road from Dover, entered the city. Continue on passing three more sites of Roman towers coming down to street level and the site of St George's Gate. The gate was named after the street which went from Westgate across the city and had many uses including a prison, a store house and an ammunition house, finally being demolished in 1801. Cross over St. George's Street on to Burgate Lane which is the continuation of the medieval ramparts coming to Burgate, another Roman gateway where the road from Richborough entered the city. Through its illustrious history the gateway was associated with a chapel dedicated to St Michael but by 1516 the church had been dismantled and only the tower remained until 1684 with the last of the south wing being brought down to widen the road in the 1800s. From Burgate turn right and sharp left coming out onto the main road passing a car park on the left coming to Queningate. This gate was named after Queen Bertha who was a practising Christian when she married King Ethelbert and this route was her daily walk to the chapel of St Martin in the city. Now on Broad Street continue on to Northgate where a Roman gate stood over the road coming from Reculver to the city and continue on to St Radigunds Street which continues the line of the city wall. At St Radigunds Bridge the ancient wall carried on over the River Stour on three arches and after being demolished in 1769 a small single track for walkers only was built. Not until 1840 was it possible for road traffic to cross the river at this point. Further on traces of Abbott's Mill can be seen in the gardens opposite the Millers Arms. This watermill was first constructed for the abbey of St Augustine and it was also used as a granary in the Napoleonic wars before being destroyed by fire in 1933. Continue along the road into Pound Lane where both 19 and 16 incorporate a medieval bastion in the structure, then on to the infamous Roman Westgate Tower where in the Saxon period a chapel was added above the archway. In 1370 the tower was restored, taking ten years to complete, only for it to be transformed into a gaol from the 1400s to 1829. Beastly tales are told and escapes are also documented in the archives housed in the tiny museum in the tower. (Admission fee. Open Mon-Sat 11-12.30 and 13.30-15.30). Cross over the road into the Westgate gardens walking beside the River Stour where, in the far corner, is the marker where the London gate stood depicting where the Roman road built between A.D. 270-290 from London entered Canterbury. The path continues through a meadow up steps and along the Rheims Way going under the subway and coming out opposite Canterbury Castle. (An alternative flat route, retrace steps back to Westgate Tower, walk through the High Street to St Margaret's Street on the right then straight over up Castle Street coming to Canterbury Castle). Canterbury Castle was established in the 1080s replacing an earlier motte and bailey fort in Dane John, and today preservation work allows an insight into

Roman buildings as this was one of three castles in Kent. Outside the castle is the site of Worthgate where the road from Wye entered the town. From here go through an alleyway coming out to Wincheap Gate which is the entrance to the Dane John gardens and the end of an historic journey.

With Canterbury's history also come ghostly tales and what better way to 'see' these ghosts than by the Ghost Tour where, during 75 minutes, something or someone could materialise to give 'live' entertainment. (Fee charged Friday and Saturday nights all year 8pm). Another specialist tour of a more serious nature is an interest in the origins of Christianity in England, visiting St Martin's Church, this being the oldest church in England,

Westgate Tower.

St Augustine's Abbey and Canterbury Cathedral. Attractions in Canterbury include Greyfriars Chapel, a 13th century building spanning the River Stour, this being the chapel and house of the first Franciscan settlement in Britain. (Free entry, open Mon to Sat 2pm-4pm, 1st April - end Sept). The Weavers, firstly a Refectory, then used as a hall and market for selling cloths from 400 looms, where the ducking stool was used in the seventeenth century to clean the cloth in the River Stour.

In the fifteenth century pilgrims' inns, taverns and lodging houses were built to help supplement the housing for the poor. The 'Sun Tavern' is one of the very few buildings left in the city. The 'Crown' containing the 'Sandwych Chamber', its vaulted cellars, survive as Debenhams restaurant. Goldstone's Bull Inn, described as a wooden building of many lodgings, can still be seen in part in Burgate where shops have always been under the lodgings (area of Talisman and Laura Ashley). The least attractive apartments 'The Shambles' were in Butchery Lane where Liberty's have restored part of the original door and window corner.

The Eastbridge Hospital, founded following the death and martyrdom of St Thomas Becket on 29th December 1170 in Canterbury Cathedral, was used as accommodation for poor pilgrims visiting his tomb. Today the hospital provides accommodation for the elderly and is still held in great esteem by pilgrims visiting the city. Opening hours 10am - 5pm Monday-Saturday. In Burgate the Church of St Thomas stands majestically behind the remnants of the Tower Arch, where a

Statue to St. Gregory the Great.

statue stands to depict St Gregory the Great for the anniversary of the arrival of St Augustine in A.D. 597. Writers also have been influenced or resided in the city. The creator of Rupert the Bear, **MARY TOURTEL,** who was born in Palace Street, went to the Simon Langton school for girls and then trained as an artist in the Sidney Cooper Gallery of Art. She married Herbert who was an aspiring poet working for the Daily Express newspaper and illustrated a number of his poems. Herbert was asked to launch a rival comic character to Teddy Trail of the Daily Mail and Mary took on the work creating Rupert Bear. She wrote over eighty-seven stories with more than 3500 drawings. She also created Rupert's friends Bill Badger, Edward Trunk, Algy Pug, Podgy Pig and the Wise Old Goat. A shop in Orange Street is dedicated to Rupert along with the Museum of Canterbury in Stour Street. (Entry fee, open Mon to Sat 10.30am - 5pm. Sundays June to Oct 1.30 - 5pm only).

GEOFFREY CHAUCER and his 'Canterbury Tales' stories of a collection of pilgrims following the Pilgrims' Way heading for Canterbury to make penance at the tomb of Thomas Becket and pray in the cathedral. Chaucer visited the city as King's Messenger and attended the funeral of the Black Prince, brother to the Duke. The pilgrims are brought to life in an exhibition in the Canterbury Tales Visitor Centre, St. Margaret's Street.

CHRISTOPHER MARLOWE, born in Canterbury in 1564, went to The King's School and then on to university, to be eventually recruited as a government agent for Queen Elizabeth 1. While at university he began to write poetry and being a contemporary of Shakespeare became very popular in his day and was acknowledged as the father of English verse drama, writing 'Dr Faustus', 'The Jew of Malta' and others.

Tower arch.

T S ELIOT who wrote the play 'Murder in the Cathedral' based on the murder of Thomas Becket in 1170.

IAN FLEMING who created James Bond. Living for a while in Bekesbourne near Canterbury the book 'You Only Live Twice' was written at the 'Duck' public house in Pett Bottom. Another book 'Chitty Chitty Bang Bang' was based on a colourful local character Count Zborowski who lived in Bridge near Canterbury and owned a famous racing car in the 1920s.

JOSEPH CONRAD was born in Poland and became a British citizen in 1866. He lived in the Rectory next to Bishopsbourne church in his retirement. His early years in the navy provided material for his sea setting of The Nigger of the Narcissus, Lord Jim and Typhoon along with his more political writings 'Under Western Eyes' as well as the murder mystery and espionage set in London 'The Secret Agent'. The Museum of Canterbury, Stour Street, has an exhibition and features on Conrad's work. Open all year. Mon-Sat 10.30am - 5pm. Sundays 1.30 - 5pm June to October.

CHARLES DICKENS lived for many years in Rochester, Kent, but was known to be a great traveller and would often stay in the Sun Inn, Canterbury. A much read book David Copperfield, has strong connections with Canterbury.

JANE AUSTEN was a frequent visitor in the district. Her brother Edward was adopted by the Knight family who lived in Godmersham House just outside Canterbury. After the death of Mr Knight Edward took over the property and Mrs Knight moved into a house in Whitefriars in

Canterbury, where Jane often visited. Edward married the daughter of the family who owned Goodnestone Park where Jane visited and the gardens were a source of inspiration for her in her writing.

JOHATHAN SWIFT, author of Gulliver's Travels, had connections through his great-grandfather and great-great-grandfather who were both rectors of St. Andrew's Church which stood at the entrance to Mercy Lane, Canterbury.

DANIEL DEFOE, author of Robinson Crusoe and Moll Flanders, was also a preacher who came to Canterbury in 1729 to preach at Blackfriars which was an Anabaptist church.

SOMERSET MAUGHAM lived in Whitstable with his uncle and went to The King's School where memories of his school days were recorded in his book Of Human Bondage. He spent much of his adult life in France but maintained close links with King's where after his death his ashes were buried in the school grounds.

Ducking stool.

RICHARD LOVELACE, whose poem 'To Althea, from Prison', has possibly some of the most quoted lines in poetry 'Stone walls do not a prison make, nor iron bars a cage'. He was a member of an old Kentish family who owned Greyfriars, a thirteenth century building which spans the River Stour in the city centre. Canterbury also has a river boat historic trip encompassing historic buildings with picturesque natural scenery. (Starts from the Ducking Stool, Old Weavers, summer months only). Victorian horse-drawn carriage guided tour of Canterbury from Stour Street. The Canterbury Festival held every year for two weeks in October is a highlight of different activities surrounding Canterbury's history and culture with plays and exhibitions throughout the city.

Old Weavers.

TRY NOT TO MISS The Westgate Towers. Activities and displays, visit the guard chamber, climb up the battlements. Open Mon - Sat 11am - 12.30pm. 1.30 - 3.30pm. Museum of Canterbury. Apart from housing Rupert Bear and his chums, Joseph Conrad and his works, there is a space for Bagpuss which started life 30 years ago in a house in Blean where the co-author still lives. Open Mon - Sat 10.30am - 5pm. Sundays 1.30 - 5pm June - October. Admission charge. Roman Museum, Butchery Lane. Open Mon - Sat 10am - 5pm. Sundays 3 - 5pm June - October.

List of walks in the Canterbury area

East Blean Wood Reserve

This area is the most easterly part of the over two thousand year-old 'Blean' woods, which covers over 277 acres, now owned by the Kent Wildlife Trust and designated a Site of Special Scientific Interest. This semi-ancient woodland Is home to the rare Heath Fritillary Butterfly which feeds on Cow-Wheat which in turn colonises much of the ground opened up by coppicing. Many varieties of bird are seen and heard in the woods including the Nightingale, Tawny Owl, Nuthatch and the Tree Creeper along with the Woodpecker, as well as species of insects, butterflies and small mammals like rabbits and squirrels.

In its early period the area belonged to St Augustine's Abbey and was passed on to the Archbishops of Canterbury and later to the Church Commissioners. As it was once the haunt of smugglers it is easy to see why Thomas Hole in 1626 panicked as he got lost in the depths of the woods and was guided out by the bells of Herne Church. Today the area has many paths for walkers opening up a Pine plantation in the interior along with massive, and tiny, Oak trees on the outer paths and coppiced Sweet Chestnut, as well as bluebells and wood anemones.

East Blean woods.

East Blean Wood Reserve

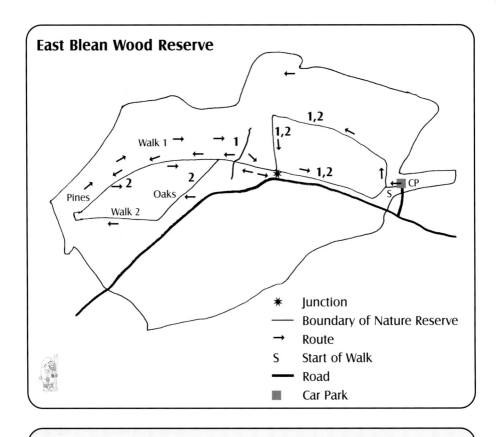

Access/Parking: Take the A291 Herne Bay to Sturry road. Turn off into Hicks Forstal Road. Follow road through woods. Car park on left.

Map Reference: OS Explorer 150. GR193644.

Distance: Walk 1. 3 miles.
Walk 2. 4 miles.

Time: Walk 1. 1½hours.
Walk 2. 2hours.

Terrain: Mud/grass paths. Slippery when wet. Woods can be very dark in the winter months. Areas of flooding in wet weather.

Refreshments: Fox & Hounds Pub, A291 towards Herne Bay ½ mile from Junction, open all day. Hot/Cold meals. Punch Tavern A291 towards Canterbury ½ mile from junction. Open all day. Hot/Cold meals.

Route directions.

Walk 1. From the car park take the path near the information board. Bear right at the junction on to a mud/grass path which leads through Chestnut and Cobnut trees, onto the main semi-concrete path. At the junction turn left and stay on the path as it winds leading round into a more open coppiced area, with tiny Oaks showing new growth. Coming to a junction by the road turn right heading down a slight incline on a grass/mud path heading through a corridor of Oak trees and thick dense bracken undergrowth. As the path flattens out notice a path leading off to the left (Walk 2). Go straight on as the path slowly climbs coming up alongside the Pine wood. Take the well-worn path on the right heading into the pine wood. Years of pine needles scatter the floor giving cover for small mammals with huge wood ants' nests dotted everywhere. Once through the pine trees the mud path carries on through dense Oak and Chestnut woods, often with a fallen tree across the path brought down by the hurricane and descends down to a small stream. Cross over the stream and staying on the path it comes out at the junction by the road. Bear left onto the well-worn bracken corridor path heading through a coppiced area of Chestnut trees, staying on this path to the junction leading back to the car park.

Walk 2. Turn left on to a well-walked mud path passing areas of Wood Anemone growing in the spring and stay on the path as it starts to climb slowly. Coming to a junction bear right, then right again, coming onto a wide grass/mud path. Carry straight on the main path going down very slowly and passing the Pine wood on the right. Stay on the path as it flattens out then slightly climbs up coming out at the junction by the road.

Return route for Walks 1 and 2. At the junction cross over onto the path directly opposite which runs alongside the road. This mud path goes through woods both ancient and young, winding and dipping, allowing more of the natural woodland to be absorbed. Stay on the path as it bears left, and then turn right at the junction as the path leads back to the car park. This area is often flooded in wet weather.

Woodland path.

Clowes Wood

Part of the ancient Forest of Blean this area of woodland tells a story of the area. The Small-leaved Lime was once dominant in the wildwood but massive clearances by the Neolithic people cleared the area and now only a few old coppice stools and saplings survive. Today the woods represent a much later chapter of the Middle Ages with its mixed broadleaved/conifer woodland including Norway Spruce, Scots Pine, Western Hemlock, Beech, Larch and Sweet Chestnut. Natural ponds and open grassland support a wide range of flora and fauna like the Yellow Archangel, Dog Violet, Woodrush, and varying fungi in the Autumn. The Heath Fritillary Butterfly is a special visitor to the area and with Nightingales, the Green Woodpecker and Tree Creepers expect to see or hear nature at its finest on that special walk.

Rest at the Winding Pond & Winding Wheel Seat, this being a natural pond where wildlife drink, insects flourish and nature abounds. The pond was first used by the steam railway company which ran its trains from Whitstable to Canterbury stopping on the hill to replenish the steam engine. This area is a main point of the Crab and Winkle Way walk.

Explore the inner boundaries of the woodland on newly created paths which delve into the inner sanctum of the woods by walking the same path as animals, picking up the various scents of the pine trees, viewing birds and insects in their daily habitats, which is both a nature lesson and experience in a walk.

Rest area, Winding Pond.

Clowes Wood

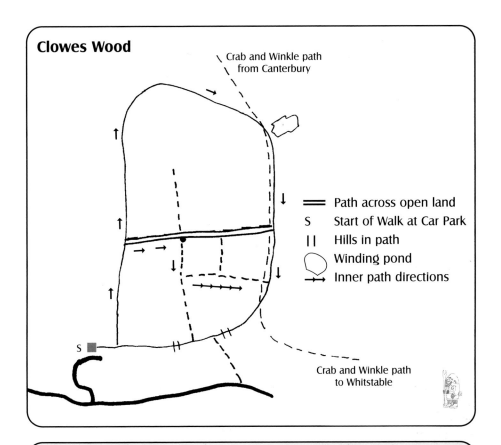

Crab and Winkle path from Canterbury

=== Path across open land
S Start of Walk at Car Park
|| Hills in path
◯ Winding pond
→→ Inner path directions

Crab and Winkle path to Whitstable

Access/Parking:	From the Rheims Way turn down London Road heading for A290. Take left onto A290 then first right. Stay on the road heading up Forty Acres Road towards Chestfield passing through Tyler Hill. After approx. 2 miles turn left at Gypsy Corner into the car park. Free parking.
Map reference:	OS Explorer 150. GR137629.
Distance:	2¼ miles outer path.
Time:	1½ hours.
Terrain:	Wide concrete path. Suitable for all. Slopes. Inner path through dense woodland, uneven paths.
Refreshments:	Ivy Public House, Tyler Hill 2 miles. Hot food midday. Open 11am-3pm. 6-10.30pm Mon-Sat. Sun 11am-3pm. 7-10.30pm. Chestfield Barn pub 1 mile from car park. Hot meals midday Mon-Sun. 11am-3pm. Mon-Sat 11-3pm. 6-10.30pm.

Route directions.

From the car park take the mud path going through an iron gate and follow a thin concrete path onto main path junction. Turn left onto the wide concrete path heading through a corridor of Oak, Chestnut and conifer trees. Keep a look out for wildlife foraging through the thick dense woodland as the path slowly climbs and a gully appears. Stay on the main concrete path passing an open area of grassland on the right noticing pylons along the path which can be used as a short cut across to the return concrete path OR the start of the inner woods paths.

INNER WOODS PATH, head along the open grassland and then turn right onto a mud uneven path heading into Pine woods. Stay on the path heading down and into deeper woodland. At the next junction turn left. The path opens up into a wide grass path coming out to the return concrete path. Bear right heading on downhill passing the Crab and Winkle junction. Continue back as main walk directions.

MAIN WALK CONTINUATION, as the path slowly climbs it bears to the right and comes up to a junction. Bear right and carry on round a wide bend coming to a notice on the left pointing out the Winding Pond and Winding Wheel Seat rest. The Crab and Winkle

path joins here (as shown on map). Venture in and absorb the tranquillity of the area where wildlife and pond life are encouraged to flourish. Turn left heading downhill on the main concrete path walking in between a Chestnut, Oak corridor with bracken, foxglove and wood sorrel covering the ground. On the right is the grass area of the short cut mentioned earlier and further down pass another exit from the woods where the inner paths join the main path. At the bottom of the hill bear right with the path coming onto the flat passing a junction on the left. (Crab and Winkle path continues on downhill at this point). Bear right as the path starts to climb and then dip, climb and dip, climb and dip, passing through dense woodland, before coming onto the flat. Carry on to the junction going straight over and into the car park.

Pathway from rest area.

Blean Meanders

Blean Woods, apart from being a Site of Special Scientific Interest, is also famed for housing the pavilion of white woollen cloth which was set up to shelter members of the royal family who visited the tomb of Thomas Becket in Canterbury Cathedral, as there was no palace to rest in at the time. Queen Margaret, wife of Henry VI, was the first to use the area in 1445 on her pilgrimage.

This area of over 11 square miles celebrated fifty years of being named a National Nature Reserve in 2003, and is part of the Ancient Forest of Blean. Being one of the largest broad-leaved woodland nature reserves in southern England it covers a large area across the belt of London Clay north of Canterbury. With a RSPB Reserve there is also a fantastic array of insects from the rare Heath Fritillary Butterfly, the odd black and orange beetle by the name of Aritus Homeopathicus and the Triplax Lacordairii beetle which only seems to like oyster mushrooms found on decaying Elm or Beech trees, to the army of wood ants, which in turn have their own eco-system. In Walks 2 and 3, after passing an area where tree planting has been happening since the storms of 1987 and a glade open area important for insects and birds, the path passes an area of open heathland (a rare habitat in Kent) which is being controlled for scrub invasion, which in turn encourages wildlife. Many more natural wonders are seen en route opening up a nature wonderland. The long walk goes through areas of woodland which encourage shrubs and flowers to grow in varying seasons, which in turn help insects to flourish, and a bird reserve where many species of bird including Hawkfinches, Yellowhammer and Whitethroat can be seen or heard, along with the rare nocturnal Nightjar.

Stream and rest area.

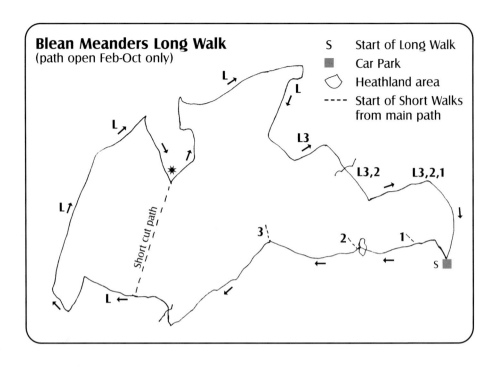

Blean Meanders Long Walk
(path open Feb-Oct only)

S   Start of Long Walk

◼   Car Park

⬠   Heathland area

----   Start of Short Walks from main path

Short cut path

L   L   L   L3   L3,2   L3,2,1   3   2   1   S   L   L

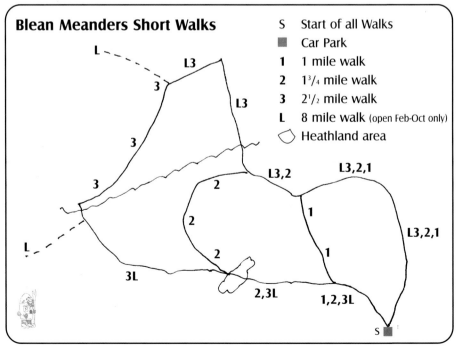

Blean Meanders Short Walks

S   Start of all Walks

◼   Car Park

1   1 mile walk

2   1³/₄ mile walk

3   2¹/₂ mile walk

L   8 mile walk (open Feb-Oct only)

⬠   Heathland area

L   L3   3   L3   3   3   L3,2   L3,2,1   2   2   1   L3,2,1   2   1   L   3L   2,3L   1,2,3L   S

Access/parking:	Take the A290 from Canterbury to Honey Hill. Turn off left to Rough Common. Turn right beside the bus stop. Follow the track into woods up to free car park.
Map Reference:	OS Explorer 150. GR123594.
Distance:	Walk (1)1 mile. Walk (2) 1³/₄miles. Walk (3) 2¹/₂ miles. Long Walk: 8 miles (Only open from Feb-Oct)
Time:	Walk (1) 30mins. Walk (2) 1¹/₂hours. Walk (3) 2hours. Long walk: 4¹/₂ - 5 hours
Terrain:	Short walks. Concrete paths, mud paths, can be boggy in summer. Steep hill on return path. Through dense undergrowth in summer months. Long walk. Concrete paths, wide grass paths, boggy areas in summer, hill on return path. Deep dense woodland.
Refreshments:	Dog and Bear pub on Rough Common Road. Open all day weekdays for food, ¹/₂ mile from car park. Local shop opposite pub open till 8pm weekdays, 6pm w/ends.

Route directions.

All the walks start from the car park going under a canopy of Silver Birch and Chestnut trees, with a dense thicket of undergrowth each side of the path.

Walk 1. Stay on the path coming to the junction and turn right. (Walk 2 bear left here) A wide grass path winds slowly downhill through dense covered woods coming out into an open area with clumps of heather on each side of the path. The twisting mud path descends heading back into the woods where it is possible to see the spectacular sight of a Wood Ant nest which can be 3ft high as it plays its part in the ecology of the area. Stay on the concrete/grass path as it goes down to a stream and back uphill into dense covered woods. Turn right at the junction onto a well worn mud path and stay on this path as it winds round and out onto the main concrete path. Head downhill to the stream and back up the hill going through a dense Oak-wooded area. Coming to a junction bear right going uphill through Chestnut woods which have created a high canopy coming out into the open. Bear right onto the path passing a bench situated in the trees and head down the canopied path created by massive Chestnut and Oak trees as it winds its way out into the open with thick low undergrowth each side and out into the car park.

Walk 2. Stay on the path to the junction. (As Walk 1) Bear left on the mud path winding through Oak and Chestnut canopied woods coming out onto an open heathland area. The Memorial Glade, a part of the heathland, was created in memory of Brian Kowesk, a local naturalist, where a bench has been placed for anyone to sit and admire the beauty of the butterflies as they dance across the heather and cow-wheat and listen to birdsong of the Nightjar and Tree Pipit. Stay on the path as it climbs very slowly passing through the heathland area, ignoring a path off to the right, which is a short cut back to the return path. Carry on past a newly coppiced chestnut area of woods on the right and bear right at the next junction. (Walk 3 bear left) Stay on the path heading into a dense canopied Chestnut woodland and go over a tiny bridge then continue along the mud path which comes out on open land. At the junction carry straight on heading back into coppiced woodland on a well worn path bearing right heading uphill on the main concrete path then downhill to the stream. Now on the main path return back to the car park following the directions from Walk 1.

Walk 3. Follow directions for Walks 1&2. Pass by the Memorial Glade, and through the heathland to the junction. * At the junction bear left on a clearly defined gravel path covered by fallen leaves, heading into dense Oak woods. Pass magnificent ants nests on the side of the path as it slowly drops down to a stream and after crossing the bridge the path climbs back up a fairly short but steep slope, all the time becoming darker as the canopy cover thickens. Stay on the path to the next junction and turn right onto a wide grass path passing by Cobnut trees with Chestnut, Holly and Oak trees lining the path with gorse and bracken undergrowth and yet more ants nests engulfing an ancient tree stump. Now the path winds and slowly descends (the long walk path joins from the left) heading for a stream where a welcome bench awaits. Absorb the view through the trees each side of the bridge as nature intended before starting the slow climb up. A junction on the right is where Walk 2 joins the return path, carry on up spotting a welcome bench on the side of a small glade. Rest and absorb the sights before continuing on up passing a junction on the right (Walk 1) and then bear right with the main path and coming along the flat gravel path to the junction, bear right beside the bench, along the path back to the car park.

Long Walk. Directions as short walks passing the junctions for Walks 1 & 2 to the junction of Walk 3. At this point turn left and stay on the grass track crossing over at the next junction, all the time looking out for different species of butterflies and insects attracted by a variety of flora. Ignore the small paths on the left and right heading back into heathland and at the next main junction turn right heading down into woodland. Carry on down to the stream then cross over and on to a concrete/mud path which goes back up a steep hill through a dense canopy of Chestnut woodland. Once at the top turn left and come on to a grass winding path which slowly climbs and go through a boundary gate. Carry on up looking out for a well worn path on the left heading into dense woods. (At this point there is a short cut path taking off about 1½miles of deep woodland and a steep climb. Comes out at point *).

Stay on concrete/grass path as it bears right and head into the dense woods on a thin mud trail noticing that the area is dark but magical with the canopy allowing chinks of sunlight to streak across the woods. Stay on the path as it slowly climbs passing through an opening beside a gate across the path. As the path bears right a wire boundary fence is visible on the left. Passing through another gate the path dips and climbs as it winds with dense woods on the right. Bear right with the path as it goes downhill then flat as it passes a stream on the left with ants nests all around, then comes out into the open and back into woodland. At the junction go straight over heading back into dense woodland and stay on the mud path coming to a concrete path. Cross over and take the mud path directly opposite going uphill heading through more open woodland, passing an open space of coppiced Chestnut trees which is a haven

Uphill path from rest area return of all walks path.

for insects. Once at the top of the hill turn left at the junction onto a concrete path. Stay on the left of the path and turn left about 50 yards along into woodland on a boggy mud path. (Even in the summer the path looks like a jungle hike with overhanging trees and overgrown foliage.) Stay on this path to the next junction and bear right beside a bench onto a wide concrete path carrying on as the path descends through thick woodland of Chestnut, Oak with the odd evergreen sprouting and all playing host to insects and squirrels. Once on the flat turn left at the next junction. Now back on a mud path heading through dense woods the path climbs steeply and then bears right coming onto a concrete path as it descends to a stream with a welcome bench in sight. Now on the main concrete path where Walks 3 and 2 join the main path from the right, pass another bench on the left, a welcome rest on the steep climb. Carry on uphill passing the 100-150 year old Oaks which create a canopy over the path giving the whole area an aura of mysticism. The path continues up and down twisting through woodland down to a stream then climbs once again. Coming to a junction turn right beside the bench and continue on uphill through dense woods coming out onto a flat mud path. Stay on this windy path with thick foliage on each side with Chestnut trees standing proud in the background. Pass another bench set in a small clearing and come out into the back of the car park.

Heathland area on short walks 2-3 and long walk.

Stream and bench on walk 3.

Denge/Eggringe Wood 'Walk on the wild side'

An ancient woodland of over 64 acres with pollard Hornbeam and in between the valleys coppiced Sweet Chestnut dominate with plantations of Conifers and Beech. On the chalky slopes a vast array of orchids like the pyramidal, greater butterfly, twayblade along with dog's mercury, cowslip, black knapweed and the very local milkwort flowers. This area is also one of the best to see the lady orchid aptly named as each flower resembles a lady dressed in a pink-spotted dress and bonnet.

With this profusion of flowers many varieties of butterflies are attracted to the area. The common blue and brown argus, grizzled and dingy skippers, green hairstreak and the marbled white and a special visitor the Duke of Burgundy fritillary. Wild privet, dogwood and other scrub encourage the nightingale, willow warbler, chiffchaff and other birds to breed.

Bonsai Bank, an area designated Site of Nature Conservation Interest, was aptly named as in the early 1900s the chalk bank was planted with Norway Spruce conifers and Red Cedar trees. In the late 1980s the area was abandoned as being uneconomical and the area named Bonsai Bank as the conifers were dwarfed due to the lack of earth and water needed for plentiful growth. (Bonsai means dwarf.) Now dwarf Norway spruce and red cedar grow in the clearings in the nature reserve. The area also attracts dormice, badgers, toads and a great variety of insects which can be seen on the paths while walking, or in the branches of the majestic trees in the woodland.

When returning to Canterbury turn right out of the car park (or left from the Compass Inn and left at the junction) and continue along the road entering a dense canopied area of Chestnut and Oak where chinks of sunlight break up the dark secretive woodland floor both left and right of the road. Then the road comes out to an explosion of sunlight and colour as it drops into the valley passing fields of crops. The contrast is both exhilarating and explosive and is a continuation of the walk experience.

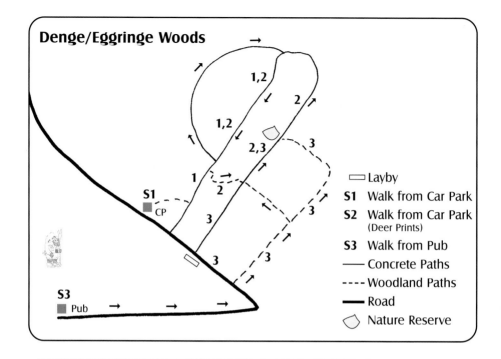

Denge/Eggringe Woods

Legend:
- Layby
- **S1** Walk from Car Park
- **S2** Walk from Car Park (Deer Prints)
- **S3** Walk from Pub
- —— Concrete Paths
- ---- Woodland Paths
- —— Road
- ◇ Nature Reserve

Access/parking: From Canterbury take B2068 towards Hythe. After 5km turn right to Petham. Follow sign to Anvil Green, and then turn right at Sole Street crossroads. Free car park ½ mile on right.

Map Reference: OS Explorer 137, 138, 149, 150. GR097504.

Distance: From car park: Short walk 2 miles. Short walk 3 miles.
From Compass Inn, Sole Street 4 miles.
Short walk: 1½ hours. 2½ hours.
3 hrs from Compass Inn.

Terrain: Short walks mud/concrete paths, steep hill. Compass Inn, road walking, concrete paths, slow hill climb, woods area possibly muddy paths.

Refreshments: Compass Inn, Sole Street 5mins from car park. Open all day. Hot and cold food. No toilets in car park.

An extra 1+ mile walk on concrete suitable for all with slow hill climb. Park in the bay beside the road, ½ mile on from either car park or junction. All-concrete path leads downhill then up to the Bonsai Bank Nature Reserve returning on the same path.(This section of walk described in Compass Inn walk).

Route directions.

Short walk. 2 miles. From the back of the car park follow a mud path bearing right going through thick woods and out into a clearing passing ancient Oaks. Continue on to a concrete path and turn left staying on this path ignoring the turning on the right. Carry on to a junction and turn left onto a mud path as it bears left heading into woods of towering Oak, Beech, and Pines with undergrowth of mosses, carpets of bluebells and rare orchids in varying seasons. Now the gravel path goes downhill passing through coppiced and ranging Beech trees and once on the flat bears right. Stay on the path to the junction and bear right going on round a wide bend. As the path starts to climb very slowly look to the left and right into the woods to catch a glimpse, possibly, of wildlife. Once at the top the path joins up at the junction taken earlier.There are two ways back to the car park, carry on along the concrete path and back past the ancient Oaks or follow the sign Car Park, heading back through a small concentrated wooded area with brambles and ditches to navigate coming out at the back of the car park. This path can be very boggy in the wet.

Short walk 3 miles. Follow directions as previous walk onto the concrete path then bear right on to a wide mud path staying on this path to the junction with a gravel path. Turn right and go along for about 20 yards then turn left heading into a thick wooded area on a well used mud path and follow the path to the end as the last 50yds drops steeply onto a concrete path. Now turn left and stay on the winding concrete path as it climbs coming onto the flat with the Bonsai Bank Reserve on the left. (*Take a detour into the reserve, follow the paths round and see the Bonsai Norway spruce along with many species of butterfly, insects and birds. It's a spectacular memorable experience). Carry straight on (or turn left out of reserve) and follow the thinning concrete path as it goes downhill passing a farm on the left and then passes houses as it winds bearing left coming round onto a wide concrete path. Follow the path as it climbs slowly and steeply and once on the flat follow directions from previous 2 mile walk back to the car park.

Walk from Compass Inn. After parking in the pub car park turn left onto the road and head along the road to the junction and turning left cross over the road to the right hand side staying on the road for about 1/2 mile. Look for an opening on the right into the woods staying on well-worn path as it meanders through dark, dense woods of Oak, Chestnut, Beech. The path heads to the back of the woods with cornfields seen through the trees. Stay on the path as it winds through the woods coming to a dip junction. Cross over the dip onto a much

Bonsai Bank Reserve.

thinner mud path going along the top of the ridge which allows a majestic view into the valley, possibly seeing animals or flora in different seasons. Stay on the path as it descends and bears to the left coming out opposite the Bonsai Bank Nature Reserve. After going round the Reserve turn right heading downhill on a wide concrete path and once on the flat each side of the winding path is an array of Orchids, Hogweed, Bindweed, and other flowers intermingled to give an array of colour to visiting insects. Looking into the dense woods walked through earlier squirrels and other tiny mammals might be seen. The path climbs coming out on to the road. Turn left walking up the road to the junction and then turn right heading back to the Compass Inn.

Main concrete path in woodland.

Bonsai Bank Reserve.

Crab and Winkle Walk

This walk is part of the original Crab and Winkle railway line opened in 1830 as the first regular steam railway with many distinguished names associated with it including George and Robert Stephenson, John Dixon, who helped in the construction, and William James 'the father of the railway' who drew up the plans for the route. Passengers were carried until 1931 after which the line was used for goods only, closing for good in

Section of pathway in Clowes Wood.

1953 due to lack of use and the line was either built on or became overgrown and forgotten. The Crab & Winkle Line Trust was set up in 1997 and in 1999 a path was open for a traffic-free route going through unspoilt countryside and woodland between Canterbury and Whitstable. The walk incorporates many points, starting with the sculpture 'Regeneration and Return' where the walk starts from Rough Common crossing the Sarre Penn stream then passing the earthworks which are the remains of a first to third century Roman villa. The path continues on past the ancient church of St. Cosmus and St Damian in the Blean, first built in 1230 although a church was here from possibly AD303 when the two saints, who were doctors, were martyred. Another unusual feature of the church is that it is moated, which suggests that the area could have been a Dark Age fortified site. The graveyard is said to contain the unmarked grave of Agnes Gibbs. She never grew properly and her stunted body was a curiosity to many. Queen Victoria's mother heard about the child and requested her presence in London so she could see for herself. The girl was examined by the Queen's doctor but sadly Agnes died aged just two years old and only 18 inches tall. Her father had her buried in the churchyard late at night with no gravestone so that the grave robbers could not dig her up for the surgeons to dissect.

The path continues along the Salt Way. This ancient pathway was used to transport salt from the Salt Pans at Seasalter to Canterbury as salt was a very highly valued commodity. Crossing this pathway Tyler Hill Road gets its name from the production of pottery during the 13th and 14th centuries in the area. The path then goes through a section of Clowes Wood with the Winding Pond and Winding Wheel Seat being the half way point and a welcome rest area. The water was originally used by the steam engine that wound the locomotives up the steep gradient there. Once through the woods the path goes over the New Thanet Way, opened in 1998, and on into Whitstable, a town famous for its oysters and the festival held in the last week in July, the development of the diving suit in 1828 and spectacular sunsets, which have been captured by many artists including Turner. Visit Dollar Row along the seafront which is said to have been built by the treasure found from deep sea diving.

Crab and Winkle Walk

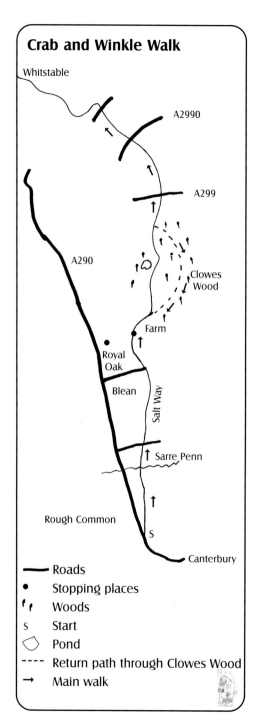

Whitstable

A2990

A299

A290

Clowes Wood

Farm

Royal Oak

Blean

Salt Way

Sarre Penn

Rough Common

S

Canterbury

— Roads
• Stopping places
↟ Woods
S Start
◇ Pond
---- Return path through Clowes Wood
→ Main walk

Access/parking: Take the A290 Canterbury to Whitstable road. Turn left at the top of the hill into Rough Common Rd. Park on the road in turnings on left.

Map Reference: OS Explorer 150. GR131595.

Distance: 8 miles

Time: 3-4 hours

Terrain: Concrete paths, steep hills, part of walk through Clowes Wood, walking in built-up area.

Refreshments: Farm shop open in the summer for cold drinks, snacks, on Salt Way path. Go left down Chapel Lane on to the main road to Royal Oak public house, open all day, hot and cold food, fruit from kiosk in the car park in summer.

Information: A **bus route** from Whitstable to Canterbury runs every hour to return from walk. **Return** from Clowes Wood section of walk to Canterbury 6 miles. **Starting point Canterbury,** from the High Street go through Westgate Towers over the level crossing and straight on up St Thomas Hill coming to the start point in Rough Common, on the right side of the road, close to University buildings.

Route directions.

After parking head back to the main road and cross over at the junction. Stay on the left hand side of the road and walk down about 50yds towards town. Look for an opening on the left where the sculpture shows the start of the walk. Passing more of the University buildings the path comes out on to a road then bears left back on to the concrete path. Going over the bridge of the river Sarre Penn carry on past the earthworks and the church onto the section of the ancient 'Salt Way' path which passes fields of crops and breathtaking views of the countryside. Stay on the path as it slopes down then climbs coming out onto the flat then passing an apple orchard on the right and on past the farm shop, where goods are for sale and heading back out into the countryside. Stay on the path as it passes between crop fields and a farm house on the right and at the junction cross over the road (Tyler Hill Road). Carry straight on along the path directly opposite as it twists passing open fields on the left and stay on the concrete path as it bears right heading into Clowes Wood where Pines, Oak, Ash and various flowers flourish. At the junction go straight on downhill seeing on the left the Winding Pond rest area which is a welcome sight (Pond and downhill path mentioned in Clowes Wood walk.) Continue down the hill bearing right with the path looking out for the junction on the left which carries on downhill. [At this junction bear right to return to Canterbury by Clowes Wood coming round to the Winding Pond rest area and retrace path.]

Stay on the path as it descends, going through a boundary gate and on downhill, coming out of the woods onto the flat then climbs as it crosses over the new Thanet Way (A299) where conservation by the side of the road has allowed wildlife to flourish. Carry on along the path as it climbs heading towards houses, on through the estate and out on to a road where bear left coming to the main road. Cross over the main road via the bridge then passing the cemetery carry on downhill passing the railway station and shops ending up by the harbour wall.

Path exit heading to Whitstable.

Section of pathway in Clowes Wood.

Stodmarsh Nature Reserve

This area on the bank of the Great Stour river covers more than 241 hectares of marshland supporting important rare wetland birds like the Bittern and the Bearded Tit. Reed beds are rare throughout the country and this is the largest area of reed beds in the southeast, making them a Site of Special Scientific Interest and an area of Special Conservation. The earliest recorded use of the land was by the Augustinian monks who dug ditches to bring the river floodwater onto the meadows which were used for grazing for mares in foal and was then known as Stud-marsh. Time changed the name to Stodmarsh. By the early 1930s subsidence was noted in the area after Chislet colliery was opened up at the beginning of the century. Small lagoons formed and reed beds developed spreading over the land resulting in the area of marshland seen today. The extensive reed beds and lagoons are probably similar to what the area looked like before it was drained and the monks dug the ditches.

Apart from an abundant bird life the lagoons have a profusion of fish and insects along with a number of dragonflies, including the uncommon Hairy dragonfly and the rare Twin-Spot Wainscot moth. These together with water voles, water shrews, weasel, stoat and fox are all seen at varying times in the reserve.

Grove Ferry a thousand years ago was under water, with the Wantsum Channel cutting across the fields separating Thanet from the mainland. In some parts the channel was three miles wide allowing shipping to enter the Thames, but with the channel slowly silting up large areas of marshland regularly flooded. The Little Stour was dug as a drainage channel in 1562 from Wickhambreaux to Plucks Gutter as a final attempt to keep the Wantsum navigable. The Grove Ferry Inn beside the Great Stour river dates from the seventeenth century and was rebuilt as a staging inn in 1831 between Herne Bay and Dover. The pub has long associations with the ferry which was until 1964 the only way to cross the river. In the seventeenth and eighteenth centuries smuggling was rife in the area.

With one of the ferrymen in with the smugglers, if the excise men were chasing them the ferryman would go to bed so the excise men could not cross the river to give chase, and the contraband would be lowered into the river to avoid detection. The pub owns a licensed boat which goes up the river in the summer months. Fishing is permitted. (Enquire at the pub for details of both). It is also possible to hire a boat in the summer time (Enquire at the boat yard opposite the pub).

Stodmarsh Nature Reserve.

'Grove Ferry', Stodmarsh Nature Reserve

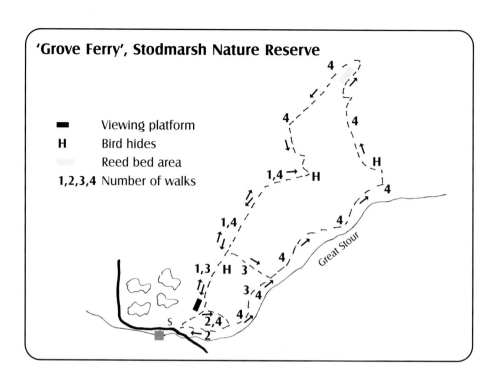

- ▬ Viewing platform
- **H** Bird hides
- ▨ Reed bed area
- **1,2,3,4** Number of walks

Stodmarsh Walks

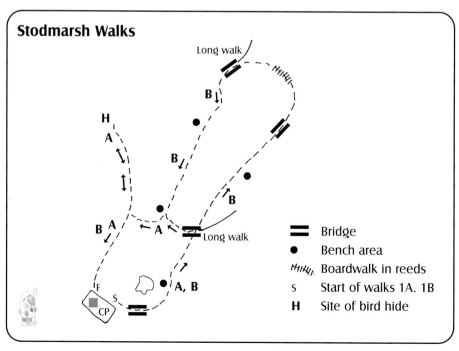

- ▬▬ Bridge
- ● Bench area
- ⅲⅲⅲⅲ Boardwalk in reeds
- S Start of walks 1A. 1B
- H Site of bird hide

Access/Parking:	Take the A28 (from Canterbury) to Grove Ferry. Cross the railway line, then the river, car park on the right on bend. Parking in pub car park. Stodmarsh village off A28. Parking area beside the track by the Red Lion pub.
Map Reference:	OS Explorer 150. GR235633.
Distance:	Stodmarsh (1A) $^1/_2$ mile. (1B) $^3/_4$ mile wheelchair access paths. Grove Ferry (1) 1 mile wheelchair access path. (2) $^1/_2$ mile. (3) 1 mile. (4) 5miles complete reserve.
Time:	Stodmarsh (1A) 30 minutes. (1B) 45 minutes. Wheelchair access. Grove Ferry (1) 40 minutes. Wheelchair access path. (2) 20 minutes. (3) 40 minutes. (4) 3-3$^1/_2$ hours.
Terrain:	Stodmarsh - wheelchair access paths, boarding, slight uphill/downhill gradients, may need help. Can be boggy in wet. Grove Ferry - wheelchair access paths. Can be boggy in wet. Reserve - grass paths, uneven surfaces, bridges, styles, concrete paths, fields which are often boggy.
Refreshments:	Stodmarsh - Red Lion pub. Grove Ferry - Grove Ferry Inn. Open 11am-3pm 6-11pm Mon-Sat 12noon-10.30pm Sunday. Bar food daytime. Main evening meal. Outside picnic area in the summer.

Route directions - Grove Ferry Walks - route numbers 1, 2, 3, 4.

(1,2,3,4) From the car park cross over the road on to a gravel pathway and follow the pathway round passing woodland on the right and stay on the concrete path coming to an information board. (2, 4) At the junction just before the board turn right onto a gravel path (muddy in the winter) walking through a meadow where wildlife can be spotted at any time. (2) Turn right onto a grass then a concrete path with the Great Stour river on the left and follow it round and back to the road opposite the pub. (4) Turn left onto a grass path walking beside the Great Stour. (1, 3) At the information board junction go straight on passing on the left a viewing mound (up a short steep slope) which from the top gives a fantastic view across reed marsh areas and Feasts Lake, Roger's Lake, Veal's Lake as well as Burnham's Lake where the migratory and wetland birds nest and in the summer dragonflies and moths can be seen. Well worth a stop if possible. Carry on down the main path which now is grassier coming to Fields hide on the right. (1) At the hide retrace the path back past the mound and the information board heading along the concrete path to the road. (3) Carry on along the track to the next junction where turn right and turn right again at the river walking beside the Great Stour on a grass path. At the next junction carry straight on coming back to the road

The Great Stour river.

opposite the pub. (4) Carry on along the grass path beside the Great Stour river passing a junction on the left and coming to a bench. Stop to take in the views across the meadow. Stay on the path passing overhanging weeping willow trees, their branches dangling daintily in the swirl of the river, grasses and ferns, all attracting various insects. A small stream appears on the left where ducks and other birds are often heard but rarely seen as they use the cover of the reeds and grasses. As the path winds the scenery changes as the reed marshes are now clearly visible over to the left with another bench in a strategic position allowing a clear view. Stay on the path as it bears left passing a private harbour on the opposite side of the Stour and continues round following the contour of the river for a short time, and then bears left heading away from the river. Passing a bird hide on the right stay on the path and look out for a tiny inlet on the right where soil erosion has created a mini bay looking out over a large expanse of water. The view from the bank or the bench at the top of the inlet is spectacular in all seasons. Carry on along the path coming to a turning on the left (part of Walk 1B) and go down the slope onto a wooden bridge which continues on to a boardwalk and into the reed beds. It is an exhilarating feeling to be so close to nature and perfectly safe being on the edge of Kent's largest reed bed with a population of rare Bearded Tit, which depends on this habitat for its survival. After crossing another bridge the concrete path continues through woodland with a bench situated in a pleasant position as to be able to view the flora and fauna in the area. Coming to the next bridge cross over and turn sharp left on to a grass path with a stream on the right. Heading through woodland gaps in the trees reveal open fields and a farm on the right and then houses come into view. Coming to a small bridge cross over and turn left into a field. (Cattle may graze at certain times, be wary of an electric fence on the left.) Walk through the field which can be boggy even in the summer and turn left with the well-worn path into another field heading towards two bridges. Cross over the bridges and turn left on to a grass path walking beside a stream. (This path can be boggy). Passing another bird hide on the left turn right and continue along the grass path escorted by 7ft high grasses each side then bear left with the path coming to a gate. Go through the gate, cross over the path and back through the gate opposite on to a grass path with a stream on the left. Stay on the path as it bears

Boardwalk through reed beds.

round and passing a bridge on the right carry straight on to the next bridge. Cross over coming into a field and carry straight on to the next bridge admiring the variety of flowers and insects en route. Go over the bridge out on to a concrete path and junction. Turn right then 1st left on to a concrete, grass path and follow it round bearing right as it passes open lakes on the left. Passing a hide on the left continue along the path passing the raised mound on the right and back to the road.

Stodmarsh walks (1A) (1B) Both walks start from the car park.
(1A) From the car park bear right on a concrete path and before crossing a bridge look out for a pond on the left where insects and plants seen in the reserve are also here. Coming to a second bridge turn left and carry straight on passing a bench then turn left at the next junction. Continue on noticing a turn on the right which leads up to an easy access bird hide set in the reed beds, then return to the main path and continue straight ahead back to the car park. (1B) Follow the directions to the second bridge then turn left and immediately right climbing a step onto another footbridge and heading into woodland of Alder, through willow scrub and onto the boardwalk which goes through the reed beds where the rare Bearded Tit can be seen at close quarters. This path allows the walker to be at one with nature, an experience never forgotten. Coming up a slope onto the bridge turn left at the junction staying on the concrete path passing a bench where the view into the woodland across the stream is worth a stop. Carry on to the next junction, bear right then next left and stay on the path as it leads to the back of the car park.

View across Reserve.

The Stours Explored

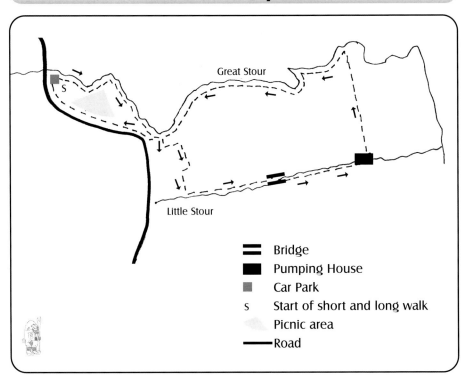

Great Stour

Little Stour

Legend:
- ≡ Bridge
- ■ Pumping House
- ■ Car Park
- S Start of short and long walk
- ▲ Picnic area
- ▬ Road

Access/parking:	As Stodmarsh Nature Reserve. Parking in the picnic area car park 50p a day Monday-Saturday. £1 Sunday & Bank Holidays.
Map reference:	OS Explorer 150. GR235633.
Distance:	Short walk 1 mile. Long walk 5 miles
Time:	Short walk 30+ minutes. Long walk 2+ hours.
Terrain:	Short walk: grass path slightly uneven, grass. Suitable for all, an area to experience all of nature. Well worth the walk. Long walk 2 stiles 2 bridges, as short walk, concrete paths, fields which can be boggy in wet weather.
Refreshments:	Grove Ferry Inn. As Stodmarsh Nature Reserve walk. Toilets in picnic area car park.

Route directions.

Short Walk. From the car park walk into the picnic area car park bearing to the right, where a path leads up a short slope onto a grass path beside the Great Stour river. Stay on this path following the contour of the river all the time absorbing the beauty and tranquillity of the area. Often private boats can be seen moored on either side of the river along with fishermen sitting waiting for that 'special' catch. Coming round the bend notice a gathering of boats of all shapes and sizes in a small marina, then as the path slopes down bear right passing a gate and head towards the back of the grass area. Follow the contour of the trees walking on flat grass taking in the beauty of flowers, insects and birds seen. Over to the right the river bank walked on earlier is visible in all its glory. Carry on the grass path heading back into the picnic area car park.

Long Walk. Directions from the car park as the short walk to the gate. Go through the gate out on to the road but do not cross over. Turn left go up the road 20 yards and turn right going through a metal gateway. Stay on the well trodden path heading up the side of the field and at the junction bear right staying on the path passing two farm buildings. (This is a section of the Stour Valley/Saxon Shore paths). Stay on the path going round the edge of fields coming to a gateway. Bear right heading round the edge of the field then left, then 20yds on, right going over a bridge and continue round the edge of the field walking beside the Little Stour river. At the bridge go over and turn left at the base of the steps on the other side onto a thin path beside a crop field. Stay on this path heading for the building ahead which is a pumping station. Climb over the style onto a concrete base then over the style opposite and turn left passing the pumping station. At the junction turn right then 20 yards on bear left on to a grass path passing a field boundary of hedgerow bushes. Stay on this path as it winds through fields, (ignoring side turnings) then passing dykes on the left where bulrushes help hide birds, ducks and many insects. The path then goes up a short slope coming out to the Great Stour river. Turn left and follow the contour of the river on the grass path coming to the back of the marina. At the junction carry straight on the concrete path coming to the metal gateway passed through earlier. Turn right go along 20 yards then through the gate into the picnic area and follow the directions for the short walk back to the car park.

View along Little Stour river.

Pathway beside Little Stour river heading to pumping station.

Pathway beside Great Stour river.

Perry Wood Extraordinaire

This woodland of 150 acres is both steeped in history and a haven for wildlife as well as its trees being used for traditional crafts. 'The Pulpit' situated on top of 'The Mount' at 504ft is the highest point in the woods and gives a magnificent view over the surrounding villages of Kent. 'The Mount' has been a significant landscape feature since prehistoric Mesolithic flint tools were found in the area when it could have been used as a defensive site. More recently it is thought to have been part of the Cinque Ports semaphore telegraph between Deal and the Admiralty in London. An Iron Age earthwork dominates another section of the woodland.

Coppicing is the ancient way of managing woodland, which is still actively practiced in Perry Wood. The main tree is Sweet Chestnut which is a hardy wood used for fence posts, palings and hop poles. When the small tree is cut down it soon sends new shoots straight up from its base, but while it is rejuvenating the woods surrounding the area benefit as light can reach the forest floor encouraging new plants to grow. The plants like bluebells, sage and foxgloves attract insects such as butterflies and beetles to the area. In time the tree grows up looking like a shrubbery which in turn attracts birds like the Blackcaps, Yellowhammers, and Nightingales which are attracted to the Chestnut coppice. Once the trees are grown and are creating a dense canopy a new area of coppiced land starts the cycle once again. Beech and Oak trees are also well established in the area along with an area of Conifers en route up to The Mount where the tops of the trees create a dark canopy overhead and pine needles adorn the floor giving a rich carpet for insects to flourish. Out on the top of The Mount lone pines stand against the wind surrounded by bracken with a small ring of conifers in a round on the top which acts as a beacon seen from other hill tops. Noticing the pebbled path on the way up and down from The Mount it looks as though it is a false path to help with drainage in wet weather, but no, the stones are a natural phenomenon caused by a geological strata called the Oldhaven Beds and found only occasionally in Kent. Wildlife such as badgers, stoats, voles and foxes all inhabit the woods living off nature's table. The whole area is a wonder of nature to be admired, absorbed and respected as a place to remember with Walks 2 and 3 climbing up on to The Mount and visiting The Pulpit allowing a part of Kent history to be included in your exploration of the area.

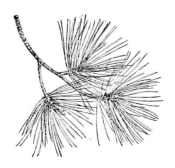

The Pulpit.

Pathway up The Mount.

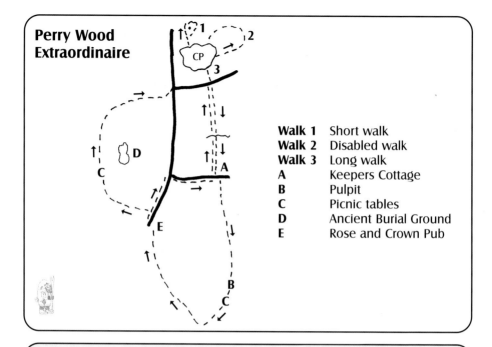

Perry Wood Extraordinaire

CP

Walk 1	Short walk
Walk 2	Disabled walk
Walk 3	Long walk
A	Keepers Cottage
B	Pulpit
C	Picnic tables
D	Ancient Burial Ground
E	Rose and Crown Pub

Access/parking: From the Brenley roundabout at the M2, A2, A299 intersection take the junction to Selling. Turn left, then right passing hop fields on right. Bear left down to junction. Turn left. Stay on road for 2 miles passing the Sondes Arms pub on left. 3rd junction on left turn going uphill. At crossroads turn left, car park 50 yds on left.

Map Reference: OS Explorer 149. GR045557.

Distance: (1) Short walk ¼ mile. (2) Short disabled walk ½ mile. (3) Long walk 3+ miles

Time: (1) 15 - 25 minutes. (2) 25 - 45 minutes. (3) 1½ - 2 hours. These times are only a guide, depending on how many stops are made to absorb the views.

Terrain: (1) Mud paths, slope down and climb up. (2) Mud/sandstone flat path, care needed in wet weather. Guide rail all the way round. (3) Mud paths, road walking, steep climb up to The Mount. Steep descent, aided by steps through woods.

Refreshments: Rose & Crown Perry Wood. Open 11am-3pm. 6.30-11pm Monday to Saturday. 11am-3pm. 6.30-11pm Sunday. Hot food served midday and evening except Sunday & Monday evenings.

Route Directions.

SHORT WALK (1) In the car park go to the back taking the path into the woods to the left of the picnic site passing a log at the entrance. Carry on ahead going through a canopied tree line with cobnut shells underfoot, then bear right with the path heading into a clearing. Take the left fork heading downhill on a mud path with tree roots forming part of the path. Coming out of the woods the path passes a fenced area on the left and a pond on the right. Carry on down to the bottom of the hill then bear right crossing a bridge over the pond and stay on the path as it climbs winding with the contour of the pond. Look out for fish and other insects which flourish in this tiny oasis of wooded wonder. Carry on up the mud path through woods coming out into the clearing started from earlier. Head straight on then bear left with the path coming out past the log at the entrance to the car park.

SHORT DISABLED WALK (2) Go to the information board, just to the left, and look for a wooden fenced rail which is the guide/support rail. This is the start of a $^1/_2$ mile tour of wonder allowing all to enjoy and absorb nature's secrets. Head into the woods on the wide sandstone path with bracken and Buckthorn each side of the path. Heading deeper in, the grass mud path is canopied by Beech and Chestnut trees which in turn give cover to many species of bird living in the woods. Stay on the path as it bears round to the left, still with the guide rail, passing in the deeper woods lichens, moss and mushrooms in autumn, on the floor and growing off stumps as well as bracken, brambles and woodland flowers in the seasons. Listen and look out for squirrels and birds in the canopy while small mammals may scurry across the path as they can often be heard but rarely seen. Carry on round staying beside the guide rail as the grass mud path comes into more open wood with Chestnut and Oak trees giving a canopy as the path comes out behind the picnic area.

LONG WALK (3) Come out of the car park crossing the road and take the path directly opposite heading uphill on a concrete/sand path with leaves and mushrooms cushioned on each side of the path. Coming out onto the flat notice the trees thin out after going through a Chestnut tree canopy which gives shade in the heat but can be dark in the winter. Carry on down the path going into a dip crossing over a dried up stream on a wooden boardwalk and climb back up the hill coming to a junction with the Keepers Cottage gate on the left. Go straight over the concrete path heading back into a Conifer wooded area and staying on the mud path this is the start of the steep climb up on to The Mount with tree roots and pine needles scattered across the path acting as steps. On the way up, and reaching the flat, look across at the spectacular view of the Conifers as the path has climbed through the trunks of growing trees and reaching the top are the tops of the trees from the bottom. Once on the flat carry on through the Conifers going down a slight dip then straight on ignoring paths on the left and right. (Paths on left and right are a short cut back down The Mount to the path going round the base of The Mount). Carry on up the hill coming out into the open on a stone pebbled path with bracken each side. As the path slowly climbs, views across

Ancient burial mound.

the valley to the east and west are impressive with the east showing off the Chartham Hills and the southern part of Canterbury, the north showing the sea and Whitstable while the west has Lees Court, a seventeenth century architectural wonder. Staying on the path still climbing notice a clump of Pines on the right, just past these The Pulpit comes into view straight ahead. After climbing up onto The Pulpit and absorbing the views, go round to the back passing picnic tables and chairs and continue on the path heading down a steep slope with wooden steps woven into the path to aid descent through a bracken corridor. At the bottom bear right going up a slight slope heading through a canopy of Chestnut trees. (Now on path going round base of The Mount). Stay on the mud path as it winds passing Chestnut coppiced trees on the right and fenced open fields on the left and continues on passing fungi settled in Chestnut trunks with the odd Holly bush giving a

Pebbled path up to The Mount, geological strata called Oldhaven beds.

dash of bright colour. As the path winds and slopes down passing a garden on the right bear left onto the road, passing a memorial tree laid out for Bishop K Warner 1891-1983. Carry on along the path coming out beside the Rose & Crown pub.

FROM THE PUB 2 ROUTES BACK. (Route 1) With the pub behind you turn right walking up the road looking out for a gravel path leading off to the right. Go along this path 200yds coming to a junction. Turn left going down into a dip over the boardwalk back up a slight slope and back down on the sand/concrete path to the road to the car park opposite (path as start of walk to Keepers Cottage gate). (Route 2) With the pub behind turn right heading up the road and turn left going uphill on a tiny stoned path beside a wooden fence heading into woods. Carry on climbing coming out on to the flat and a picnic area where the views across the valley are again well worth the climb. Carry on along the flat on a pine needle path looking across through the Pine trees at views of parts of Faversham and the Isle of Sheppey. As the path starts to descend it curves round an ancient earthworks which is now being slowly eroded by children riding bikes. Stay on the path as it winds slowly descending, wandering through thickets of woodland and bracken undergrowth and leads out to the road. Turn left, go along 20 yards, then turn right and along 50 yards to the car park.

View from The Pulpit across the valley.

Rose and Crown pub.

Fordwich and 'Swan Lake' Explored

Fordwich, known to be one of the smallest towns in England, has a wealth of history to its name. Fordwich was the medieval port for Canterbury being the highest navigable point on the River Stour. Its name appears in the Domesday Book as one of the eight boroughs in Kent with its land owned by the abbot of St Augustine's Abbey. In the thirteenth century a port was built to unload food for the monastic people and stone for the rebuilding of Canterbury Cathedral which was brought up from Sandwich Bay. Mayors were elected every year to uphold the law and they tried cases in the little Court Hall then drowned thieves just opposite in the Stour. Today, the Town Hall (court hall) with its gaol on the lower floor and a jettied upper room of timber and brick and tiled roof, along with a black boarded shed which housed the town crane for unloading, was at the opposite end of the bridge to the toll house. The Town Hall is one of the focal points there opposite the Fordwich Arms, and going through a narrow winding street of town houses the George and Dragon pub was the toll house, being on the opposite end of the bridge. St Mary the Virgin church nearby the Fordwich Arms is a small, mainly thirteenth century church with a tall shingled steeple and box pews, a solid wooden penitent's stool along with a rare chancel arch, a tympanum with the arms of William III and the Ten Commandments, a celebration of the Glorious Revolution of 1688.

The lakes with reeds and overhanging Willow trees are the remnants of flooded holes left after the excavation of sand and gravel. The reed beds and wet grasslands surrounding the lakes provide homes for many water birds and wetland creatures and winter time sees large numbers of swans and ducks gathering. On one lake in particular the swans are seen with their young, where they can be heard taking off and landing often noisily across the water. This is a serene area of natural beauty and flat paths for all to enjoy.

'Swan Lake'.

Fordwich and 'Swan Lake'

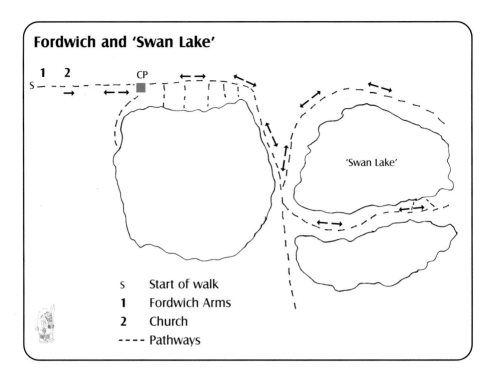

s   Start of walk
1   Fordwich Arms
2   Church
- - - -   Pathways

Access/Parking:	From Canterbury take the A28 to Margate and turn off in Sturry village to Fordwich. Go over the bridge. Road winds passing the George & Dragon pub. (Can park in car park and follow road on foot to church). Go through the town and then straight on (road bears left). Parking in Fordwich Arms car park or beside the road opposite.
Map Reference:	OS Explorer 150. GR181597.
Distance:	3 miles +
Time:	1½ hours +
Terrain:	Flat walking, concrete paths, grass paths.
Refreshments:	Fordwich Arms 11am-3pm Monday-Sunday. Hot and cold food served. 6.30-10.30pm Monday-Sunday. No hot meals.

Route directions.

From the Fordwich Arms walk down beside the church on a concrete path passing houses on the right and continue on going through a swing gate. Walk through the car park and straight on passing a small lake on the left and the start of a larger lake on the right. Stay on the main concrete path as it bears right going around the edge of the lake (look out for small paths on the right meandering through the trees brambles and reeds, each heading down to the edge of the lake). Walking beside the lake absorb the spectacular natural sights of the many species of water bird including the Tufted Duck, Eider Duck and Moorhen, insects including damsel flies, skaters and the sight of fish 'jumping' through the water along with small islands situated discreetly on the water line. Reaching a junction carry straight on then bear left after 20yds heading along a concrete grass path.

EXTRA WALK Bear sharp left at the junction heading along a grass path into reeds, brambles and Willow trees with a small lake on the left and the start of a large lake on the right. Staying on this path it winds through a dense canopy passing a spectacular growth of foliage which is often part of the path with small paths heading to the edge of the lake. Due to dense growth the path has become overgrown and unusable so after an area of open reeds where the swans are seen in all their glory (this is Swan Lake) return by the same path back to the junction and continue on 20 yards then bear left with the path.

CONTINUE along the grass path passing between two lakes both of which hold sights and sounds of natural beauty. The path meanders along coming to another overgrown area where it is not possible to continue on but before that point a path on the left on the bend leads through a tree line to the lake where a bench is placed discreetly allowing fantastic views of both Greater Bladderwort plants and their brilliant yellow flowers (in season) along with the swans to be seen (this is the other side of Swan Lake). Return along the same path back to the junction and then carry straight on back along the concrete path taken earlier taking in all the natural habitat around returning to the car park and through the gate back to where the walk started.

View across first lake.

Fordwich Town Hall.

View across lake.

Ashford Town

Ashford dates from long before the Norman Conquest and has been an important market town since the 12th century. A Roman road which was used to transport iron ore from the Weald to the Kent coast ran though the area but there is no evidence of occupation in any numbers. For several centuries the area was called Esshetesford and many debates could never come to the conclusion of the origin of the name but in 1085 Ashford was named in the Domesday Book as having a church and mills. In 1243 the first weekly produce market was held every Saturday with annual fairs at the end of August and by 1671 markets were allowed to sell animals. By 1856 the original market place had outgrown itself so a new site in Elwick Road was set up, now closed up. In 1861 a new corn exchange was built next to the cattle market keeping all the farming industry together, but this was demolished in the 1970s.

Ashford has played its part in history with local people playing a role in the rebellion of 1450 against the corrupt administration of Henry VI which was led by Jack Cade. Many locals were eventually pardoned but Jack Cade was killed at Heathfield in Sussex. In 1554 many locals supported Sir Thomas Wyatt, the Younger, who tried to overthrow Queen Mary but failed and were burnt alive as heretics. One man, Richard Brown, whose father had died by fire many years earlier, was saved from his fate by the death of the Queen in 1558.

Ashford grew slowly with the markets playing a central role and by the turn of the 20th century developments were taking place which laid the foundation of the town as it is today. Quality printing gave the town a reputation which others envied with the Headley Brothers renamed Invicta Press and then Geerings in 1932. Other prominent names like Charles Haywood & Sons, who produced bicycles and who in 1907 gained momentum as the 'Onward bicycle' was launched and later there was Charles Norman and his brother who produced the 'Norman Nippy Moped'.

Electricity came to the town in 1926, water was first supplied in 1905, the Picture Palace opened in 1911 and Ashford was one of the few areas of Kent to have a cinema but with no electricity. Between the wars expansion and development opened up more parishes within Ashford and The Warren area was acquired as an area of major importance.

In November 1842 the railway industry was formulated in Ashford with the first railway journeys running from Ashford to London. Five years later a line to Hastings had been established. A railway works was set up in 1847 first making steam locomotives and carriages then going on to diesel. A devastating blow came in 1981 when it was learned that the railway works were to be closed down by 1984. Now Eurostar and the high speed link from London to Europe has put Ashford on the map again. Ashford has another string to its bow, that of being one of the first towns to be twinned with Germany after the war and has been recognised as an example of international friendship, with the Rhineland town of Bad Munster Eifel. Ashford also has a fair number of buildings and roads named after famous people like Simone Weil Avenue, after the French authoress who had sympathies with the poor and worked as a labourer to experience working class life. Developing T.B. she was brought to the sanatorium but insisted on eating the same rations allowed the people so she soon died and was buried in Bybrook cemetery. Elwick, William, Francis, Jemmett and Bond Roads can all be traced back to one of the towns most successful businessmen, George Elwick Jemmett and family, who first moved to the area in 1770. The last recorded family member was W. Jemmett who was the manager of Jemmetts Bank which merged with Lloyds Bank in 1902.

Magazine Road has a military connection but nothing to do with guns. In 1797 it was where the mounted units were stationed and stores were kept for the army. Wallis Road is named after Dr. John Wallis who became a highly respected mathematician and admired by Sir Isaac Newton amongst others. Boys Hall Road in Willesborough suburb named after Thomas Boys who built Boys Hall as a family home in 1916. Also in the area a new housing development has Luckhurst Road, Woolmer, Jarvis and Shepherd Drives, Julien Place, Knott Crescent, Ealham, Cowdrey and Johnson Closes after the 1970s Kent cricket stars along with Underwood Close in Kennington suburb of Ashford.

The Brabourne family are one of the oldest names in Kent with Lord Brabourne producing such films as A Passage to India and Death on the Nile. His wife the Countess Mountbatten of Burma is an active patron of many charities. Patricia Mountbatten is first cousin to Prince Philip and third cousin to the Queen. Although part of the royal circle, all are committed to the local community. Lord Brabourne is part of the Knatchbull family who in 1486 purchased Mersham-le Hatch as their home, which is now the Caldicott Community, a foundation for the care and teaching of severely damaged children. The 2000-acre estate is still used as a top class game shooting area for the royals.

List of walks in the Ashford area

Ashford Warren

This area, although surrounded by houses and roads is known as a wildlife oasis. Within its borders is an area described as a hidden garden with exotic laurels, Rhododendrons and bamboo.

A pond area which attracts unusual wildlife encourages water birds, amphibians, damselflies, pond skaters and the uncommon water violet to flourish. Ancient Oaks, Sweet Chestnut and Silver Birch trees enhance the area and with coppicing help to create a haven for foxes, rabbits and other small mammals. Sheep's Sorrel and Bird's Foot plants thrive on the acid grasslands, which in turn bring species of butterfly into the area.

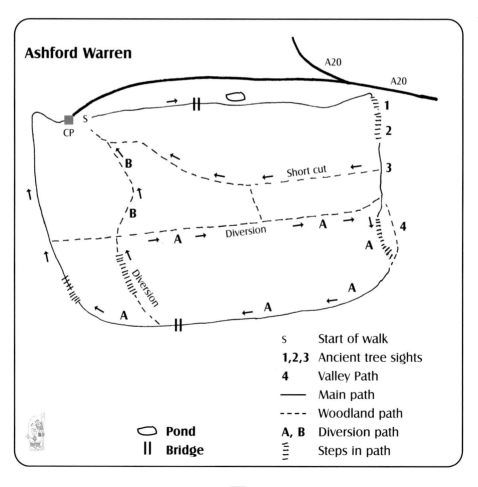

S	Start of walk
1,2,3	Ancient tree sights
4	Valley Path
——	Main path
- - - -	Woodland path
A, B	Diversion path
⦚	Steps in path
◯ Pond	
‖ Bridge	

Access/Parking:	At the A20 roundabout just outside Ashford go straight over onto Maidstone Road then take the first left on to Warren Lane, following the sign to The Warren down the road to the car park on left. Free parking.
Map Reference:	OS Explorer 137. GR004442.
Distance:	4 miles.
Time:	2 hrs.
Terrain:	Concrete paths. Mud paths. Steep climbs and descent aided by steps. Sand/gravel paths.
Refreshments:	Ashford town 1 mile.

Route directions.

From the car park walk back to the pathway near the main entrance and go along a flat concrete path through Oak and Sweet Chestnut trees passing under a bridge, with grass paths on the right leading up into the woods. Stay on the concrete path coming round to pond on the left. *Take a diversion around the pond where damselflies, skaters and many other insects live, along with various fish, and look out to the middle of the pond where a tiny island allows ducks and other birds to nest in total peace and safety.*

Once back on to the concrete path continue on as the path slowly climbs then changes to mud winding through dense Oak and Chestnut trees and continues on coming out onto open grassland and then bears to the left. Now turn right heading up a steep incline aided by wooden steps hewn into the ground. A little way up the first of the ancient Oak trees presents a magnificent sight on the left, with a bench in front and further up the stepped hill path the second ancient Oak presents its own aura. Many fallen trees lay strewn across the woods - Willow, Silver Birch, Oak and Chestnut allowing wildlife to flourish and fungi to grow enhancing the natural wonder of the area. Before reaching the top a small path on the left leads off down onto the valley floor. Stay on the main path and at the top it turns sandy (muddy in winter) as it follows the contour of the valley passing open grassland. [Look for a path off to the right heading across the grass towards trees going downhill as this is a short cut back to the car park.] It then starts to descend with steps hewn into the ground, coming on to the valley floor. (At this point a detour into the valley is an added nature bonus.) Bear right staying on the sandy path and pass under a bridge going through woodland as it curves round. (Diversion - Look out for the path on the right heading up into the woods and steps hewn into the ground to aid the climb.) Stay on the main sandy path as it winds through ancient woodland and spectacular floral displays in the summer months,

Pathway through woodland.

passing an underpass on the left, bear right with the path as it climbs with the aid of man-made mud steps hewn into the ground. Reaching the top of the hill bear right with the path as it winds through more open woodland and starts to descend, with other paths branching off back into the woods, head downhill towards the grass track and bearing left the car park comes into view.

Diversion - (A) Turn right heading up the stepped path going through denser woods. Near the top a mud path joins this path from the outside path on the left. Once on top of the ridge turn right heading along a scant mud path through dense trees climbing over stumps and jumping over tiny fissures formed over many years. The path leads back to the top of the valley where the stepped sand path goes downhill into the valley. Follow the directions of the outer path going past the diversion taken earlier heading up the stepped path and back to the car park.

Diversion - (B) Once on top of the ridge carry straight on over the top of the hill on a clearer mud path. The path then descends slowly going through thickets of dense woods and joins up with the outside path which comes out onto an open grass area where nature can be seen in the summer in all its glory, then bear left on the mud path which leads back to the car park.

Play insects. King's Wood.

King's Wood

At the beginning of all the walks is a welcome created from the forest of some of the creatures possibly seen on the walks - a treasure for all to experience. The grasshopper and the snake sculptures are just two of the many 'play' pieces of sculpture along with the wasp, the pig and the fox chasing rabbits. The nightjar and mushroom sculptures are a resting place to remember.

Starting at Farnham, in Surrey, the North Downs Way path weaves its way through Kent finishing in Dover. This 153-mile ancient path opens up a wealth of history, exploring the landscape and discovering fauna and flora, and has long offered inspiration to many writers and artists. The southern path passes through King's Wood on the 7 mile and $5^1/_2$ mile walk, where the path meanders through dense woods of chestnut and oak. Deer are sometimes seen and, through chinks in the tree line, views across the Downs open up an array of colour from the flowers, insects and butterflies in summer. On this short section of path the nature lesson leaves the walker in awe of its beauty and majesty.

Seating area at beginning of walks.

King's Wood

This area was historically a royal hunting ground for Henry VIII, with lots of small woods interspersed to create a vast area of coppiced Sweet Chestnut, Larch, Beech and Spruce plantations which are managed for timber production and, more importantly, conservation. The area has a large herd of Fallow deer running free within the 1300 acres of land along with badgers, foxes and other small mammals, as well as many species of bird like the Green Woodpecker and the rarer Nightjar. Many species of butterfly feed off the variety of wildflowers including Wood Sorrel and Foxgloves as well as the rarer Columbine, Common Spotted Orchid and Deadly Nightshade. Paths through the woods open up the beauty and diversity of the area while not disturbing the wildlife.

Another feature of this area is the Stour Valley Art Project, which is a series of sculptures drawn from the natural landscape creating art which works with the environment. All the walks pass the first area of large wooden birds, insects and other woodland features which can either be used as seating or a play area for children. The three mile walk includes more of the art projects including the Coppice Cloud Chamber, which is a camera obscura, a device which brings the outside in. This sturdy igloo-style structure is made from thousands of chestnut branches which allow the sky and treetops outside to be reflected in. Viewed both on a bright or dull day it gives an air of mysticism to the area. Another of the useful sculptures is 'The Walkway' where the path, although on a hill, is permanently wet and people have made artificial pathways around the area. The sculpture is a permanent pathway on the ground so that walkers pass each side of the wet fertile area. Other sculptures include a forty metre-long charcoal line linking a chalk circle and cone which echoes the space between the Beech trees where it can be seen. Another more poignant sculpture for the millennium is a forty metre-long avenue of Yew trees planted by many local people to view the setting sun. They are positioned in such a way that as the trees mature they will hold a vision of time of a millennium of sunsets. On the long walk the path passes a clearing where bird boxes have been strategically placed to view the inhabitants in the area then on to the North Downs Way path which passes through a park where deer are free to roam.

Coppice cloud chamber on medium/long walks.

King's Wood Walks

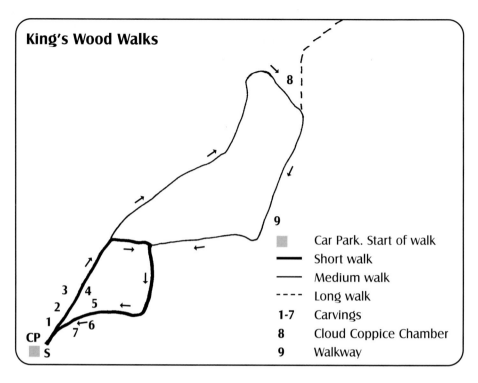

■	Car Park. Start of walk
▬	Short walk
──	Medium walk
----	Long walk
1-7	Carvings
8	Cloud Coppice Chamber
9	Walkway

Long Walk, King's Wood

1	Cloud Coppice Chamber
●	Junction Diversion Walks
A	Diversion 5 miles
B	Diversion 5½ miles
L	Long walk 7 miles
▦	Nesting box area
----	Medium walk

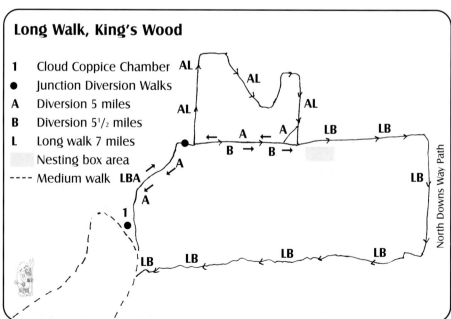

Access/parking:	Take the A251 Ashford/Faversham Road. Approx. 1 mile south of Challock take the Wye road and park (free) $1/2$ mile on left of White Hill.
Map Reference:	OS Explorer 137. GR023500.
Distance:	Short walk 1 mile. Medium walk 3 miles Long walk 7 miles (Diversions 5miles, $5^1/2$ miles)
Time:	Short walk 45 minutes. Medium walk 2 hours Long walk 4-5hours (Diversions $2^1/2$- 3hrs)
Terrain:	Short walk. Mud paths, downhill slope, uphill climb, concrete path. (Wooden sculptures) Medium walk. Mud paths, through woods, steep slopes. Long walk. Mud paths, through woods, steep slopes, concrete paths, grass paths.
Refreshments:	Challock village 1 mile. Halfway House Pub, children's play area, takeaway food, eat in. Open all day every day.

All the walks start from the car park and pass the first set of wooden Sculptures and return by the last section of the short walk.

Route Directions.

Short walk 1 mile. From the car park walk down well-worn path coming to the 'play' insects in the woodland and picnic tables further on. Stay on the well-worn path walking downhill past an open coppiced Chestnut area and at the bottom stay on the path as it bears left. Can be very muddy here. Going through the woods the path comes out onto a concrete path. For all longer walks carry straight on. SHORT WALK turn right staying on the concrete path to the junction at the bottom of a dip and turn right onto a mud path. Stay on this path walking beside coppiced Chestnut trees and ancient felled trees formed into unusual shapes. Near the top of the path notice one of the group of 3 sculptures to the right. Bear right as the path passes the three sculptures and leads up between open Coppiced Chestnut trees and carries on up the hill to the top. Bear right with the path as it goes into more densely coppiced Chestnut trees. Once on the flat look out for an ancient 'lone Pine' tree on the left of the mud path and stay on this path as it twists through the woods coming out into the complete open field area walked through earlier but further over. Stay on the path as it climbs passing more wooden play creatures and leads back up to the car park.

Medium Walk 3 miles. Follow the directions as short walk to the concrete path. Cross over and continue down a wide mud path which leads through an area of conifers which can be very boggy even in summer. The winding path leads into Beech woodland where many fallen trees are left to decay and return to the forest floor which allows insects and wildlife to flourish. As the path bears right it crosses a concrete path and heads back into the woods and down a steep slope. Now turn left at the bottom onto a wide grass path. Stay on the path for about ¼mile and then look out for a well-trodden path leading up on the right. This path is curved and sloped so aiding the climb to the top. At the second bend look over to the left to see a building looking like a log hut which is the Cloud Coppice Chamber. Carry on up the slope until on the flat and bear right at the junction. (The more overgrown path on the left is the start of the long walks).Stay on the path walking through coppiced Chestnut as it winds then descends to a concrete path. Cross over heading back into an Evergreen extravaganza, on a mud path. As the path starts to climb a 'sculptured walkway' is in position to cross a 'soak' area. Carry on up the hill to the concrete path where a welcome bench waits for those tired legs, now turn right and stay on the concrete path as it winds and descends coming to a junction at the bottom of the hill. Turn left coming onto a concrete path as it winds then slowly descends passing coppiced Chestnut on the left. Coming to a junction at the bottom of the hill turn left. As SHORT WALK. Stay on the mud path as it climbs then turns right passing the clearing where an 'Untitled Group of Three Sculptures' stand and allow wildlife to live in amongst its foliage. As short walk back to the car park.

Long Walk 7 miles. DIVERSION WALKS (A) 5 miles. (B) 5¹/₂ miles.
Follow directions for SHORT/MEDIUM walk to the top of the hill near the Cloud Coppice Chamber. Turn left going on to the more overgrown path. Stay on the mud path as it winds its way through thick bracken, open woodland and between a Chestnut coppiced area on the right heading into a more densely wooded area. Come out onto the concrete path junction.

Long Walk 7 miles. (A) 5 mile diversion. At the junction turn right heading uphill then bear over to the left and take the thin mud path going down into woodland. Follow this path all the way down to the valley floor then turn right onto a wide grass path and stay on this flat path to the next junction. Bear right, going uphill on a grass path which can be extremely muddy. Evergreen trees break up the view through the bracken as the twisting path climbs then bear right at the top of the hill. At the junction bear left, still climbing, heading through dense woods. As the path leads round a bend and starts to descend, look out for a bird watchtower at the bottom of the hill. Turn right passing the tower coming onto a wide grass path going down an Evergreen corridor and then come up to a junction.

TURN LEFT FOR LONG WALK. TURN RIGHT FOR DIVERSION WALK (A).

Diversion Walk (A) 5 miles. Turn right and go to the top of hill on the concrete path then cross over and carry on the concrete path as it winds coming back to the junction on the left coming out of the woodland. Follow the path back through the woods, coming out on the path above the coppice chamber. Turn left and follow the directions of the medium 3 mile walk (Stay on the path walking through coppiced Chestnut as it winds and descends to a concrete path) back to the car park passing the soak and wooden sculptures.

Diversion Walk (B) 5¹/₂ miles. From the junction turn right onto the concrete path as it slowly climbs up, then at the junction cross over and head downhill. At the bottom the main path off to the left is the evergreen corridor. Carry on going uphill.

Long Walk 7 miles. Turn left heading uphill on a wide path passing by coppiced Chestnut, Oak and Ash. Coming onto the flat, over to the right in an area of cleared trees, is a wildlife paradise with bird nesting boxes and a hide where they can be watched without being disturbed. Carry on along the path as it dips into a valley and go straight over at the junction heading back uphill with a Pine wooded area on the left passing the characteristic floor covering of needles and branches. Once at the top turn right. This path is a section of the North Downs Way. Stay on the grass/mud path as it winds through deep woods with fencing on the left and in between the tree-line gaps outstanding views across the Wye Valley are visible along with deer. As the path descends bear right and stay on the path as it slowly climbs back up. Turn right on to a wide grass path half way up and go round a locked gate slowly climbing. Once on the flat the path bears left winding through coppiced Chestnut trees and comes to a junction. Cross over on to a grass/mud path passing a locked gate. Now in deeper woods stay on the mud path as it winds going up, then down, and at the bottom of the hill the path comes to another junction. Go straight over back uphill staying on a mud/grass path as it winds through deep forest. As the path starts to descend look out for an opening on the left. Turn left onto the path going through the evergreen extravaganza on the medium walk. Come up to the Soak walkway and follow directions for the short route back to the car park.

Winter view along pine path, medium walk.

Play insects, short walk.

'Group of three' untitled sculptures at end of all walks.

Hothfield Common

Hothfield Common is the remnant of an ancient heath and is also a special Nature Reserve as it has the last four valley bogs found in Kent which in turn help rare bog plants to flourish. The yellow flowering Bog Asphodel, the Heath Spotted Orchid with its tiny pink-flowered spikes in mid-summer and the insectivorous round-leaved Sundew, which traps unsuspecting insects in its leaves and then absorbs nutrients from its prey. The heath also supports areas of common heather and cross-leaved heather which give the area an exceptional purple carpet in late summer. Another sight not to miss is the fluffy white heads of the Cotton Grass dancing majestically in the wind in the summer. The area is also good for reptiles including the slow worm, common lizard and grass snake along with mammals like foxes, mice, voles and badgers. Many of the insects are more rare like the Keeled Skimmer Dragonfly, which only lays its eggs in shallow acidic pools, and a Sand Wasp which takes live, but paralysed, prey back to its sand hole for the wasp grubs to feed on. The outer rim of the Common has sections of woodland which in turn attracts a range of birds like the Nuthatch, Green Woodpecker and, in the summer, the Tree Pippit which can be seen perched on an isolated tree. Livestock are present on the Common at certain times of the year to help with the conservation of the open areas.

View across the Common.

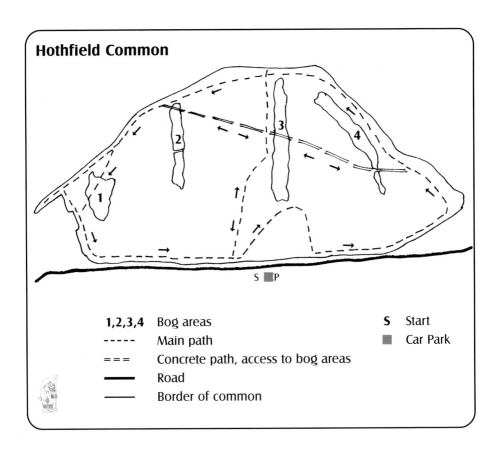

Hothfield Common

1,2,3,4 Bog areas
`-----` Main path
`===` Concrete path, access to bog areas
━━━ Road
── Border of common

S Start
■ Car Park

Access/parking:	Take the A20 from Ashford for 3 miles. Pass sign saying Hothfield on left. Bear left into layby and left into Cade Road, free car park on left 20 yds.
Map reference:	OS Explorer 137. GR973457.
Distance:	3 miles
Time:	2 hrs
Terrain:	Grass paths, uneven mud path by stream, heath and mud paths boggy in the wet. Slope uphill. Suitable for all ages over heath.
Refreshments:	Ashford 3 miles. Toilets in car park. Garage $1/2$ mile from turning. Woolpack (Beefeater restaurant) $1/2$ mile.

Route directions.

From the car park cross over the road, go through the gate and on to the Common. Bear right following the path down through Birch trees coming out in front of the heath. Stay on the path etched out by many feet as it bears to the right and follows a boundary fence line going round the outside edge of the Reserve. Stay on the path as it bears left coming round into woodland. The kissing gate on the left leads on to the concrete path which crosses the bogs 2,3,4, allowing access with no damage to wildlife. Carry on straight ahead going through woodland where the path becomes much thinner and follows the contour of the stream on the right. Climbing over roots and then a man-made bridge of logs continue on the path passing on the left bog 4 seen through the trees. Stay on the path as it winds through the woods passing the edge of bog 3 and passes another kissing gate on the left which gives access to the concrete path mentioned earlier. Carry on round the outside path which now goes through a pond with a series of upturned logs, stones and planks acting as a bridge helping to keep dry feet except in the winter or flooding. Once over the bridge stay on the path passing houses on the left and bear left with the path passing another kissing gate on the left which leads out onto the concrete path crossing the bogs. Staying on the outside path pass a cattle grid and bear left with the mud path as it climbs into woodland of fallen and still growing Chestnut and Oak. Follow the path round as it goes via a causeway across bog 1. Now in thicker woodland the path bears left uphill with deep gullies on the right formed through erosion and time leaving the area looking like a dirt track. Still slowly climbing the path bears right coming round to the top boundary fencing. Stay on this path heading through woodland which then opens up to the junction. Bear right heading uphill through the trees to the road.

Short walk through the bogs. From the car park follow the path through the trees and on to the heath. Follow the main well-used dirt path through the grass and heather heading downhill towards the woodland, coming on to the concrete path. Turn right and carry on to the end of the path and bog 4, then retrace steps and walk to the opposite end of the path coming to the main bog 2 where in the summer months Bog Asphodel, Orchid and Cotton grass are all seen as well as insects and mammals which all play a role in the bogs' survival. Retrace path winding through the heather back uphill to the car park.

Photo of Bog Asphodel growing in Bog 2.

Bog 3 looking out on to the Common.

Path leading to boardwalk crossing bog 2.

Cotton grass growing in summer.

Orlestone Forest

The Orlestone Forest is a designated Site of Special Scientific Interest where a leisurely stroll can turn into an adventure or an exploration for the rare species.

Walk 1. This area is a part of the broadleaved forest with an exceptional area of Evergreens dominating the far corner. In the summer months many species of butterfly and moth and other insects thrive on the plants and shrubs encouraged to flourish on the sides of the pathways, which gives the walker the unenviable feeling of walking in nature's garden. A complete contrast to the summer is the bleak but powerful aura of winter with various fungi underfoot, squirrels hunting for food and tiny snippets of life seen under the forest floor.

Walk 2. This part of the forest is again a broadleaved forest going through separate woods of Oak, Beech, Pines and Willow, where gorse, ferns and brambles are more abundant as the forest has a denser canopy, cutting out many plants but allowing various fungi to grow in the damp ground and on fallen trees. In the midst of the forest, off the main track, a small area of land has been designated a Nature Reserve which allows many species of butterfly and other insects to flourish.

Fungi growing.

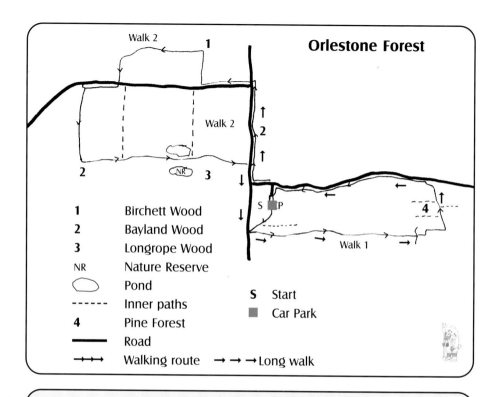

Orlestone Forest

1	Birchett Wood
2	Bayland Wood
3	Longrope Wood
NR	Nature Reserve
⬭ Pond	
------	Inner paths
4	Pine Forest
▬▬▬	Road
→→→	Walking route → → →Long walk

S Start
▪ Car Park

Access/Parking: From Ashford take the A2042 towards Kingsnorth keeping straight on at a roundabout onto Ashford Road and, later, Hamstreet Road. After approx. 5 miles turn right into Birchett Lane. Take the first turn left and right into car park.

Map Reference: OS Explorer 125. GR986348.

Distance: Walk 1. 3miles.
Walk 2. 4miles. (Long walk 7 miles)

Time: Walk 1. 1½ hours
Walk 2. 2hrs. (Long walk 3½ - 4 hours)

Terrain: Walk 1. Grass paths, concrete path. Steep climb up, slippery in wet weather. Road walking.
Walk 2. Grass paths, slippery in wet. Concrete path, road walking. For a memorable often breathtaking long walk start on walk 2 and continue on walk 1 at the road junction instead of heading back to the car park.

Refreshments: Hamstreet village 1mile.

Route directions.

Walk 1. From the car park turn right and head towards the trees and a well used path, staying on this path as it goes through a corridor of Oak trees. Bear right with the path and come out to a junction then turn right on the concrete path heading towards a gate and the road. [At this point Walks 2 and 1 join as long walk]. With the gate behind head straight down the concrete path passing open clearings of coppiced Chestnut where brambles and ferns are growing each side of the path encouraging wildlife to flourish. In the summer months butterflies and other insects accompany every step giving the illusion of walking with nature, an experience not to be missed. Stay on the path as it winds and slowly descends coming to a stream where on the right in a small clearing a bench allows fantastic views in the spring and summer months of many woodland flowers which create carpets of colour, and in the autumn fungi show off their distinctive colours. Cross over the stream then up the slope on a grass path to the junction passing a large ancient Oak tree on the right. Turn left and go along the grass path to the next junction. Turn left again onto a wide grass muddy path with Evergreens dominating the area creating an eerie but natural feel from a canopy of broken light, with needles and cones forming a cushioned floor giving a complete contrast to the earlier part of walk. Stay on the path as it climbs, ignoring paths off to the left and right. Coming out onto the flat stay on the path as it thins out with brambles each side. Follow this path to the road and turn left following the road round the bend passing a house on the corner and continue on along the road seeing the car park entrance on the left further on.

Walk 2. From the car park walk out on to the road and turn left then right at the junction. Turn left at the next junction by a house and stay on the right hand side of the road for about ½mile coming to a gate and a gravel path on the right. Go along the path passing brambles, ferns and other flora which attract butterflies and other insects allowing nature to accompany every step, especially in the summer months. At the next junction turn left staying on the concrete path passing coppiced clearings on the left and right which encourage new growth. Turn left at the next junction staying on the concrete path as it thins out coming to the road. Either climb over the mound on to the road or look to the right 20yds before the mound, a path leads through the trees out on to the road. This section of the walk is a wildlife extravaganza. Cross over the road and turn right walking along the road heading around the bend. By the notice board a path over a mound leads on to a wide grass track, or 20yds further on an opening on the left bears left and round to the grass track. Follow this more overgrown grass path as it leads down into Bayland Wood. Bear left at the junction on to concrete/mud path heading into more dense woods of Oak and Willow with gorse and bracken tendrils reaching out on to the path. Coming to a junction carry straight on along the concrete path. As it bears to the left notice a cleared area of Pine trees on the left and just up on the left, as the path bears to the right, branches of trees hide a small natural pond which in the summer months attracts damselflies, beetles, floaters and other insects as well as being a water hole for the animals of the forest. Standing still and quiet luck can allow you a sight to wonder at. On the left of the pond a dirt track leads into the Nature Reserve. Just past the pond bear left on a wide grass/mud path and admire the variety of insects and butterflies that live amongst the high brambles, trees, ferns and gorse, as you navigate the uneven path. Once at the end climb over a small mound out on to the road and turn right heading back along the road to the junction. Turn left, the car park is 100 yards on the right.

Long Walk. Continue on along the road past the turning and carry on 500yards to the gateway on the left. Continue down the concrete path as Walk 1 crossing the stream, coming up past the pine arboretum and out onto the road turning left and heading back to the car park.

Pine area Walk 1 and extended walk.

Hamstreet Woods Reserve

This area of woodland is the last remnant of an Ice Age forest. If the earth could give up its secrets or the trees talk the tales told would be of prehistoric creatures roaming the land looking for food and water. Entering the woodland of Oak, Ash, Hornbeam, Birch and Aspen trees, all showing off their natural beauty, as well as a sprinkling of Wild Service trees, captures the essence of the area. Discreetly within the area of 230 acres is a National Nature Reserve of 40 acres where natural regeneration is the key to the preservation of the wild flowers which encourage birds and insects to thrive. Marsh Thistle and Rosebay Willow herb are found alongside edges of rides which encourage butterflies from spring to autumn. Dragonflies, the December Moth, along with other insects, small mammals, including the Dormouse, and animals such as the fox, badger and mole all flourish in the surroundings. Siskin and Sparrow hawks are seen flying overhead.

Pathway Walk 2 heading in woodland.

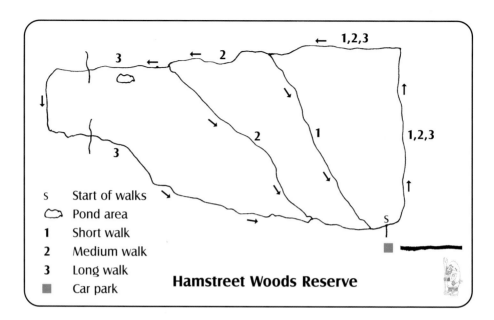

S   Start of walks
🗘   Pond area
1   Short walk
2   Medium walk
3   Long walk
■   Car park

Hamstreet Woods Reserve

Access/Parking:	Take the A2070 from Ashford towards Hamstreet village turning left just outside into Ashford Road. Turn left at Dukes Head pub. Turn off 2nd left, sign Bournewood. Free parking at the end of the road. Can get congested.
Map Reference:	OS Explorer 125. GR004338.
Distance:	Short walk 1 mile (1) Medium walk 2 miles (2) Long walk 3 miles (3)
Time:	Short walk 30 - 40 minutes (1) Medium walk 1+ hour (2) Long walk 1½ hours (3)
Terrain:	Short/Medium/Long walk. All start with a mud path steep climb. Mud paths. Grass paths. Concrete path. Woods can be dark in winter. All three walks start from the same point and fan out into deeper forest returning on the same path for the last 5 - 10 minutes.
Refreshments:	Hamstreet village shops ½ mile. Dukes Head Pub ¼ mile. Open all day, hot and cold food served. Garden for children.

Route directions.

Short walk (1). Go through the entrance gate crossing the stream and head straight on uphill on a wide mud path passing coppiced Chestnut areas each side of the path. Stay on the path as it curves then comes out onto the flat then starts to descend into a dip junction. Turn left onto a grass path and carry on past a coppiced Chestnut area on the left. At the next junction go straight over and stay on the path as it descends slightly and continues through woods. At the next junction bear right on to a mud/grass path heading into a much denser area with gorse, brambles and ferns enveloping the path. At the next junction turn sharp left. Walks (2) and (3) bear right. Stay on the wide mud path as it descends through dense woods coming to a dip junction. Walk (2) meets here. Go straight on a wide mud path heading slowly downhill, through dense woods with fallen trees, woodland plants and evergreens breaking up the gloom in winter. Bear left coming out on to a concrete path which is a section of Greensand Way path. Stay on this path passing fields to the right and a stream meandering through the tree line, and woods to the left as it bears round and crosses the bridge coming back to the car park.

Walk (2). Follow the directions of route (1) to the junction then bear right and go along 50yds then bear left going uphill into more dense woodland of Oak, Chestnut and Beech. As the mud path climbs look up through the tree line, in the winter months the bare branches allow any rays of sunlight to reach the floor and the trees seem to dwarf you against their grandeur, whilst in the summer months dense foliage gives a welcome corridor of shade. Once on the flat bear left at the next junction. Go straight on for Walk (3). As the path descends into thick woods on a well-trodden path it can be muddy in parts where the sun rarely reaches the ground and moss-covered tree trunks are evident, mixed in with the odd holly bush, giving greenery to the bare winter landscape and mixing in with the gorse in the summer. Once on the flat coppiced Chestnut trees are on both sides of the path. Bear left at the next junction on to a grass path where Walk (3) path meets up. Carry on to the next junction and turn left onto a grass path with small ridges formed in the path as it goes downhill and ends up in a dip. Turn right onto a wide mud/grass path as it meanders along a corridor of gorse, ferns and brambles backed by coppiced woods, to the junction and turn left. Now on a concrete path with the woods to the left and a stream on the right, this path is part of the Greensand Way, carry on heading back to the entrance and the car park.

Walk (3). Follow the directions of Walks (1) and (2) to the junction mentioned. Carry straight on heading downhill on a grass path passing a pond on the left which encourages various water birds and insects in the summer and then on down into a dip crossing over a stream and head back uphill bearing left with the path. At the top look out for a welcome bench on the right. Once rested carry on uphill bearing left going through woods of Chestnut and Oak and coming to a main junction. Turn left heading slowly downhill noticing mounds of dead cut wood which has been left to nature to dispose which gives a small insight into the workings of the forest insects and fungi. Look out for the stream on the left as the path still descends, then cross the stream at the bottom and climb back up on a mud path. Once on the flat carry straight on to a V shaped junction, (Walk (2) joins up here on its return) and continue on to the next junction. Turn left going down the small ridged grass path then turn right and follow directions of Walk (1) back to the car park.

Pathway on Walks 2 and 3 heading uphill, where trees dwarf the person.

About the Author

WALKS IN ASHDOWN FOREST

Christine Baldwin

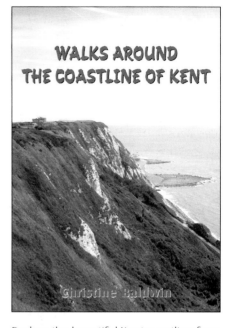

WALKS AROUND THE COASTLINE OF KENT

Christine Baldwin

Explore this beautiful area of Sussex with 23 circular walks. To enjoy the forest during all the seasons of the year select a short walk, ramble, or a day's trek. Each walk describes the places of interest, the terrain and the locations of pubs, restaurants and tea rooms.

Explore the beautiful Kent coastline from Whitstable to Rye in East Sussex, with over 20 varying walks in length. Enjoy the contrasting scenery from fossilised beaches, exquisite natural cliff formations, ancient Roman historical sites and Nature Reserves. Places of interest are included with each walk, along with pub and refreshment stops.

Christine Baldwin was born in Farnham Surrey where she attended school followed by college in Windsor. She now lives in Kent where she enjoys the sea and countryside close by. She has travelled around Scandinavia and Europe enthralled by the spectacular scenery encountered while walking which inspired her to share her experiences with others by writing The Little Hiker series of books.